SUPPRESSION
OF THE MUSLIMS

US POLICY AND THE MUSLIM WORLD

SUPPRESSION
OF THE MUSLIMS

Mohammed
Ashraful
Haque

ARCHWAY
PUBLISHING

Archway Publishing books may be ordered through booksellers or by contacting:

Archway Publishing
1663 Liberty Drive
Bloomington, IN 47403
www.archwaypublishing.com
1-(888)-242-5904

ISBN: 978-1-4808-0022-9 (sc)
ISBN: 978-1-4808-0024-3 (hc)
ISBN: 978-1-4808-0023-6 (e)

Library of Congress Control Number: 2013903674

Printed in the United States of America

Archway Publishing rev. date: 2/28/2013

Dedicated to my late parents, Alhaj Shamsul Haque and Alhaj Saleha Khatun and the fearless leader of the Muslims of Bengal: Maulana Abdul Hamid Khan Bhashani and the martyrs of genocide in Iraq and Afghanistan.

TABLE OF CONTENTS

ACKNOWLEDGEMENTS

I am greatful and indebted to Julia Allen for all her help and being patient in every aspect of this books production.

INTRODUCTION

I slam is a religion of peace, but all over the world, Muslims are portrayed as terrorists. The American media has always portrayed Muslims as terrorists. Many countries in the world have become nuclear, including Israel and India, and the American media showed no concern. But when Pakistan became a nuclear power, the American media really showed concern. I remember when Peter Jennings said on ABC, "Pakistan has detonated the Islamic bomb." Islam tolerates every religion and protects the status of minorities. When Caliph Omar entered Jerusalem in AD 634, he allowed every religion the freedom to worship. The Quran says, "God forbids you not, with regards to those who fight you not for (your) faith nor drive you out of your homes, from dealing kindly and justly with them; for God loveth those who are just" (Quran 60:8).

Islam means surrendering to the will of God. It is not a new religion but it follows the Judeo-Christian tradition that God revealed the same message through all His prophets and ended the revelation through Mohammed. Muslims represent one-fifth of the world's population. They follow a religion of peace, mercy, and forgiveness. The majority of them do not follow the concept of extremism, preemptive strikes, and terrorism. Muslims believe in one unique, incomparable God and the angels created by him. They believe in the prophets through whom God's revelations were brought to mankind in the day of judgment and individual accountability for actions, in God's complete authority over human destiny and in life after death.[1]

Muslims believe in a chain of prophets starting with Adam and including Noah, Abraham, Ishmael, Isaac, Jacob, Joseph, Job, Moses, Aaron, David, Soloman, Elias, Jonah, John the Baptist, and Jesus, peace be upon them. But God's final message to mankind—a reconfirmation of the eternal message and a summing up of all that has gone before—was revealed to the prophet Mohammed through Gabrael. Islam and Christianity do not have different origins. Together with Judaism, they go back to the prophet and patriarch Abraham, and their three prophets are directly descended from his sons—Mohammed from the elder son, Ishmael, and Moses and Jesus from the younger son, Isaac. Abraham established the settlement hat today is the city of Makkah and built the Kaba, toward which all Muslims turn when they pray.

Ever since Islam was revealed to Mohammed, it continued to spread peacefully. One of the teachings of Islam is to seek knowledge, so Muslim scholars were advancing in science, mathematics, and architecture. The United States and the Western allies—Israel, India, and Russia—have established a policy to suppress Muslims throughout the world. This alliance is also engaged in terrorism in the name of Islam to defame Muslims and increase their sufferings in everyday life.

To understand the complicated conspiracy, one must understand the relationship between the United States and Russia (the former Soviet Union), between the United States and Israel, and between the United States and India. There are 1,476,233,470 Muslims throughout the world, and out of that, a little over 252 million live in the Middle East, or about 17 percent of the Muslim population lives in the Middle East.

---

1   IslamiCity. Understanding Islam and the Muslims. Last Updated 2013.
    http://www.islamicity.com/education/understandingislamandmuslims/

There are forty-nine Muslim majority countries. Virtually none of them practice democracy. There has been no transfer of technology to any of the Muslim countries. With the blessings of the United States, Indians have penetrated every Muslim country in the Middle East. In Malaysia, Indians run the industries, and they are the technocrats. Many Indians live in Saudi Arabia, United Arab Emirates, Kuwait, and Qatar. It is clear that their intentions are to control those Muslim countries and make sure Muslims don't get any technology. To better understand this conspiracy, let us examine the US-Russia relationship first.

THE US-SOVIET (RUSSIA) RELATIONSHIP

After World War II, Europe was divided partly under Soviet Control and partly under Western Control (the United States and its Western allies). Germany was divided into East Germany and West Germany, including the city of Berlin. After the United States detonated the atomic bomb in 1949, US-Soviet relations changed. The arms race began. One should notice that there was never any direct conflict between the United States and the Soviet Union after the establishment of the Iron Curtain. There seems to be a clear understanding between the United States and Russia to divide the world and rule.

The mutual understanding between Russia and the United States goes back a long way. Prominent among those Americans who run the world from behind the scenes are the Rockefellers. After the Bolshevik revolution, the Federal Reserve and the Rockefellers tried to open up trade with communist Russia. The communist government of the Bolsheviks was saved because of aid given by Herbert Hoover.[2] Ivy Lee was the public relations agent appointed by the Rockefellers, and he tried to convince the American people that the Bolsheviks were actually benefactors of mankind. Professor Antony Sutton of Stanford University's Hoover institution made

---

2   Gary Allen, *None Dare Call it Conspiracy.* Concord, MA: Concord Press, 1971.

a distinct point in his book *Western Technology and Soviet Economic Development*:

> Quite predictably 180 pages later Lee concludes that the communist problem is merely Psychological. By this time he is talking about "Russians" (not communist) and concludes "they are all right." He suggests that the United States should not engage in propaganda, makes a plea for peaceful coexistence; and suggests the United States would find it sound policy to recognize the USSR and advance credits.[3]

After the Bolsheviks' revolution, Standard Oil of New Jersey bought 50 percent of Caucasus Oil, knowing well that Caucasus Oil had been nationalized by the Russians.[4] In 1927, Standard Oil of New York built an oil refinery in Russia, which helped the Soviet economy. It was the first US investment in Russia since the revolution.[5]

The United States continued to help the Russians. In 1927 the United States arranged a loan for $75,000,000 for the Bolsheviks. It became clear that wherever Standard Oil would go, financing was arranged by Chase National Bank, which was owned by the Rockefellers. Chase National Bank played an important role in forming the American-Russian Chamber of Commerce in 1922. Reeve Schley was the president of the American-Russian Chamber of Commerce. He was also the vice president of Chase National Bank.[6]

---

3   Anthony Sutton, *Western Technology and Soviet Economic Development, 1917–1990* (Stanford, California: Hoover Institution on War, Revolution, and Peace, 1968), 292.

4   Harvey O'Connar, *The Empire of Oil* (New York: Monthly Review Press, 1955), 270.

5   Ibid., vol. 1, 38.

6   Gary Allen, *None Dare Call it Conspiracy*. Concord, MA: Concord Press, 1971.

The Chase Bank arranged for the financing of Soviet exports to the United States and Soviet imports of US cotton and machinery. The Chase National Bank and the equitable trust company were the leaders in extending credits to the Russians.[7] However, the Rockefellers were not the only ones to finance the growth of the communists. According to Professor Sutton, "There is a report in the State Department files that names Kuhn, Loeb & Co, the long established and important financial house in New York as the financier of the first five year plan of Russia."[8] In his book, Professor Sutton proves beyond any doubt that Soviet technological developments were financed entirely by the United States.

President Lyndon Johnson appointed Rodman Rockefeller (CFR) virtually to every strategic position in his administration. Rodman Rockefeller wanted to promote trade with Eastern bloc countries and Russia. An article was published in *New York Times* under the headline, "Eaton joins Rockefellers to spur trade with Reds." The article stated,

"An alliance of family fortunes linking Wall Street and the Midwest is going to try to build economic bridges between the free world and communist Europe. The international basic economy corporation controlled by the Rockefeller brothers and Tower International Incorporated headed by Cyrus S. Eaton Jr., Cleveland financier plan to cooperate in promoting trade between the Iron Curtain countries, including the Soviet Union."[9]

The Rockefellers and Eaton built ten rubber goods plants worth $200 million. The largest truck factory in Russia was built with US financing. It built both trucks and tires. The Rockefellers and Eaton

---

7   Ibid.

8   See US State Department decimal file 811.5/3711 and 861.5 for five-year plan 1236. Sutton, op cit., vol. 2, 340.

9   Bedingfield, Robert E., New York Times, "Eaton Joins Rockefellers to Spur Trade With Reds; Cleveland and New York Financiers to Set Up an East-West Exchange Eaton Joins With Rockefellers To Press for East-West Trade." January 16, 1967.

built a $50 million aluminum-producing plant for the Soviet Union. Aluminum was needed to produce jet planes, which were considered nonstrategic, according to Johnson and Nixon. The Rockefellers and Eaton basically transferred technology from the United States to the Soviet Union.

> For five decades the communist have based their propaganda on the theme that they were going to destroy the Rockefellers and other super rich. Yet we find that for five decades the Rockefellers have been involved building the strength of the Soviets.[10]

Similarly, the United States and the Soviet Union produced propaganda against each other, but at the same time, they had a clear mutual understanding as to how to divide the world and rule.

Nelson Rockefeller never chose to run for public office, but during his time, he controlled every president in office, including Richard Nixon. It is to be noticed that the United States and the Soviet Union have gone through Cold War and have made propaganda against each other, but they have never confronted each other directly.

---

10 Gary Allen, *None Dare Call It Conspiracy* (Concord, MA: Concord Books, 1976), 107.

US-ISRAELI RELATIONS

The 1917 Balfour Declaration by the UK was considered the intention of the British to create a Jewish state in Palestine. The British gathered Jews in Palestine and in 1948 created the state of Israel. Israel was created to control and dominate the Middle East. Israel is a US satellite that is used to suppress the Muslims of the Middle East. Israel was created in 1948 in what was Palestine. Palestinians were driven out of their homeland and became refugees in other countries. This was the greatest injustice done to humanity to remove people from their own homeland. Israel has been supplied with arms and technology to be the superior military power in the Middle East. Any Middle East country that does not listen to US policy dictates will be attacked by Israel. Therefore dictators in the Middle East countries must suppress their own people.

The United States has continuously armed Israel. In 1962 President Kennedy sold HAWK antiaircraft missiles to Israel. Lyndon Johnson provided Israel with tanks and aircraft. The United States was determined to make Israel a superior power over its Arab neighbors. In 1968 Johnson cleared the sale of Phantom Jets to Israel. The United States is the primary supplier of arms to Israel.[11]

The Carter administration began strategic cooperation with Israel, which allowed Israel to sell military equipment to the United States, and the two countries had joint military exercises. Reagan

---

11 Ibid.

considered Israel a strategic ally that could contribute to keeping the Middle East under US domain.

In 1987 Congress officially designated Israel as a non-NATO major ally and allowed Israel to produce a number of defense items. Israel has been the recipient of a massive amount of US aid and grants, and their economic and military assistance continues to grow. US aid continued to pour into Israel even when Israel was building Jewish settlements on occupied territories. The United States did all this to reduce Soviet influence in the Middle East. This has always been the game plan for the United States in spite of the US and the Soviets' clear understanding as to how to divide the world and rule. The Arabs are not afraid of communism, but they are afraid of Zionism.

The strategic ties between Israel and the United States got stronger in 1997 when Israel was linked up to the US missile warning system and established a hotline between the Pentagon and the Israeli Defense Ministry. The United States continued to fund for research and development of Israeli weapons. This is a clear message to Arabs that the United States will stand by Israel to fulfill its imperialist policies.

Since 1974 Israel has received over $50 billion in US aid. Besides that, Israel has received an annual grant of $1.8 billion in military assistance.[12] Israel is fortunate to have a very influential and powerful Jewish lobby in the United States. The economic interdependence of the two countries was enhanced when, in 1984, Secretary of State George Schultz advised the creation of an American-Israeli joint economic development group (JEDG) to work toward the economic development of Israel. With US aid and grants, Israel achieved one of the world's fastest economic growth rates.

---

12 Washington Report on Middle East Affairs. "U.S. Financial Aid to Israel," Last Updated 2013. http://www.wrmea.org/special-topics/9748-us-aid-to-israel. html.

In 1996, Israel received directly from the US treasury $3 billion in nonemergency economic and military aid. The Senate passed a bill 75 to 19, and Reagan signed the first American Free Trade Agreement with Israel. The two countries have established the Binational Industrial Research and Development Foundation (BIRD)[13], which would benefit both countries in commercialization of innovative ideas. The two countries have also established the Science and Technology Commission with the basic purpose of allowing high-tech industries in both countries to engage in joint ventures and facilitate exchange of information between universities and research institutions.

There has always been an outpouring of support and sympathy for the Jews and Israel from the American people. There are no such feelings for the Palestinians, who were removed from their own homeland to create the Jewish state of Israel. This is all because of how the media portrays about the Jews and not about the Palestinians. The media is controlled by big businesses with lot of Jewish influence. Disney owns ABC, Westinghouse owns CBS, and General Electric owns NBC. "The result of the mergers is that the four major broadcast networks—CBS, NBC, ABC and Fox—are now all controlled by corporate conglomerates."[14]

The basic purpose of creating the Jewish state of Israel was to terrorize the entire Middle East. Israel continues to build Jewish settlements in occupied territories with America's blessings. In May of 1967, Israel attacked its Arab neighbors and controlled the Sinai, captured Jerusalem's old city, and on the Syrian front captured the Golan Heights, with utmost disregard for international law. Israel continues to build settlements on all occupied territories. Having no hope of getting their territories back, the Arabs, led by President

13 Gary Allen, *None Dare Call It Conspiracy* (Concord, MA: Concord Books, 1976), 107.

14 Marc A. Triebwasser, "Today's Media Conglomerates," http://www.polisci.ccsu.edu/trieb/Media.htm.

Anwar Sadat of Egypt, decided to attack Israel on October 6, 1973. But because of US and Soviet diplomatic pressure, they had to implement a ceasefire on October 25, 1973. The war caused a major shift in power in the Middle East that ultimately led to the signing of the Camp David Accords. Israel will remain a threat to the Arab world, and that is exactly what the United States planned. This is America's way of suppressing the Muslim countries.

US-INDIA RELATIONS

Ever since the British left the Indian sub-continent in 1947, India has always been blessed with American and Western support. The Indian subcontinent was divided into Pakistan and India. The provinces that had a Muslim majority went to Pakistan, and provinces with a Hindu majority went to India. However, Kashmir was 90 percent Muslim, yet the British left it disputed. Ever since India's independence in August of 1947, India has enjoyed continuous democracy and made significant progress in education, industrialization, science, and technology. Is this not because of the blessing of America?

On the other hand, Pakistan had almost continuous military dictatorship—dictators who were handpicked by America. Although Pakistan was independent at the same time as India, it is far behind India in education, industrialization, science, and technology. In public the United States always seemed to support the military dictatorship in Pakistan, but really the intention was to keep Pakistan from making progress by keeping a military dictator in power and thereby allowing India to move ahead and make progress. In India the economy is booming. The industry and service sectors are strong and growing, filled with new ideas and academic breakthroughs. Advancing modern technology and uninterrupted democratic process cannot happen without America's blessings. On the other hand, Pakistan's economy is stagnant: no advancements in technology, poor education, and continuous military dictatorship. These are all planned by the United States and the CIA to keep Muslim countries from making progress.

Until 2001, the United States has not been open about its policy toward India. During the 1971 war of independence by East Pakistan, India sided with the people of East Pakistan to form the new nation of Bangladesh. India supported the Bangladeshi war of independence because it wanted Pakistan to be broken up. America wanted the same thing, but they took the side of Pakistani military just to convince the world that it had no hand in the breakup of Pakistan, although it is my opinion that Pakistan's breakup was planned by Kissinger and the CIA.

Since 2001 the United States has openly signed many agreements with India in defense cooperation. Each month the United States and India have at least one joint military exercise with the goal of improving military operations in many areas. India has increased its military purchases from the United States. The economic ties between the United States and India have made significant progress. In terms of purchasing power, India has the fourth-largest economy in the world. Ever since it gained independence, India progressed in leaps and bounds, and its economy has doubled in the past ten years. It has skilled manpower, a very well-developed banking system, and highly trained management. It has the best education system in Asia.

Many American jobs have now gone to India. India is trying to attract direct foreign investment from the United States. The US policy has been to allow India to penetrate Muslim countries where it cannot penetrate directly or where it does not want to be exposed. In 2003, India turned down the US request to send Indian troops to Iraq. This Indian action made India look like the good guys before the Muslim world, which allowed India to penetrate the Muslim countries. This is exactly what the United States desires. India is viewed as sympathetic to the Arab world. This is the strategy that has been chosen by the United States and India. It allows Indian Hindus to deeply penetrate Muslim countries and engage in covert operations to destroy that society and keep the Muslim countries off balance.

Current US policies about terrorism are nothing but a false pretense to occupy Arab countries. Iraq had no terrorists or weapons of mass destruction. The United States decided to invade Iraq and continue its occupation. The United States actually creates and inspires terrorism.

Until recently, US-Indian relations have been such that it appeared that the United States and India were on opposite sides most of the time. Apparently that creates a very positive view of India to the Muslim world. However, the relationship that was obscured for many years has now become very open. India and the United States have entered into agreements over several bilateral issues. This includes dual-use technology. On the economic side, the United States is the biggest market for Indian products. There is a great deal of cooperation on the economic front.

The United States not only wants India to make progress but also wants to use India to counter any Chinese influence. Direct foreign investment in India is not as large as China because high-growth areas, such as software, technology, and financial support services, do not require a huge investment. However, India is attracting a lot of portfolio investment, and India can attain an 8 or 9 percent growth rate. At this rate, India could double its per-capita income in a decade.

With America's blessings, Indians have penetrated in large numbers in every Muslim country of the world, specifically in the Middle East. They go there with jobs. There are many Muslims who gain skills and are educated in Bangladesh, Pakistan, Egypt, and Palestine who cannot find jobs in the Middle East, yet Hindu Indians find jobs in the Middle East very easily. In every Muslim country, Indians run the technology. In Malaysia, the Chinese and Indians run all the industries. There are 1.4 million Indians in Saudi Arabia, a nation of 25 million. There are 140,000 Indian professionals in Saudi Arabia.

The history of the Indian subcontinent speaks for itself. Under British rule, the Hindu majority always oppressed the Muslim minority. Therefore the United States felt it would set up a policy whereby Hindus could penetrate every Muslim country, disrupt that society, and engage in clandestine operations so Muslim countries cannot make any progress in education, industrialization, or technology.

Why is the United States so bent on suppressing Muslims? American investment in India increased significantly after India's liberalization in 1991. There seems to be an increase of American interest. India had a significant growth of portfolio investment to outsiders. All the bans imposed on India because of the nuclear explosion in 1974 have now been lifted. The Bush-Bajpayee agreement signed in 2004 opened up the door for cooperation in technology. The United States has formally committed to cooperating with India in the area of civilian nuclear energy and space technology.

Cooperation on the economic front continues with business outsourcing, and American jobs are going to India. It is America's intention to make India a strong nation so Pakistan will be constantly threatened. The United States wants to use Indians to suppress Muslims all over the world. India is the Israel of Asia.

US POLICY AND PAKISTAN

When British rule ended in South Asia, India was partitioned, and Pakistan emerged as a free country on August 14, 1947. The two-nation theory emerged because Muslims and Hindus on the subcontinent constituted two distinct and irreconcilable nationalities. The Muslim minority in the sub-continent were constant victims of oppression by the Hindu majority. Therefore on March 23, 1940, the Muslim League adopted the Lahore Resolution, moved by Fazlul Haq of East Bengal. The resolutions called for an independent country for the Muslims on the subcontinent. It stated,

> The areas in which Muslims are numerically in a majority as in the northwestern and Eastern Zones of India should be grouped to constitute Indian States in which the constituent units shall be autonomous and sovereign.

Therefore, provinces in the northwest part of Punjab, Northwest Frontier Province, Sind, and Baluchistan formed West Pakistan and East Bengal, separated by one thousand miles of Indian territories forming East Pakistan.

After independence and the creation of Pakistan, the central state operatives, the military and civil service, were dominated by immigrants from North India and by the Punjabis. After independence, Liaqat Ali Khan from West Pakistan was the first prime minister of Pakistan. After his assassination, Mohammed Ali of Bogra from East Pakistan became the prime minister.

On March 23, 1956, Pakistan became a republic, with Iskander Mirza from East Pakistan as the president. However, the political role of the East Pakistanis ended with the declaration of martial law by General Mohammad Ayub Khan of West Pakistan in October 1958.

GENERAL MOHAMMED AYUB KHAN

Photo © Egon Steiner / CC-BY-SA-3.0

Political conditions in Pakistan were very unstable from its very inception. First in 1948 Pakistan wanted to impose Urdu as the national language, although 56 percent of the population spoke Bangla in East Pakistan. This caused a great deal of unrest and protest in East Pakistan by masses, students, and intellectuals. On February 21, 1952, police opened fire on students who were protesting the imposition of Urdu as the only national language. Several students died, and eventually the ruling class in Pakistan agreed to restore both Bangla and Urdu as the national languages.

DISPARITY UNDER PAKISTANI RULE

The disparity between East and West Pakistan began with the imposition of martial law by General Ayub Khan in 1958. Although Bengalis of East Pakistan made up 54 percent of Pakistan's population, they made up less than 10 percent of Pakistani ruling structure. Bengalis were less than 10 percent in industrialist, military, and civil service. Although Bengalis were 54 percent of Pakistan's population, in the military they represented only 10 percent. The Bengalis as a nationality were not adequately represented in the civilian administration or the military high command of Pakistan. The following table shows the distribution of civilian posts on the basis of nationalities.

CENTRAL GOVERNMENT CIVIL SERVICE (1955)

POSITION	EAST PAKISTAN	WEST PAKISTAN
Secretary	0	19
Joint Secretary	3	38
Deputy Secretary	10	123
Asst. Secretary	38	510

Source: Dawn, Karachi (1955)

The above table shows that although East Pakistanis made up 54 percent of the population, they were significantly underrepresented in the central government. Therefore the outlay of development funds were always much higher for West Pakistan. Once General Ayub Khan declared martial law, the industrialists were all from West Pakistan. East Pakistan was a market for West Pakistani products at a higher price than the world market. Therefore, East Pakistan was always economically exploited by West Pakistan. West Pakistan, which consisted of four provinces of Punjab, NWFP, Sind, and Baluchistan, always received more funds for development than the more-populous East Pakistan

DEVELOPMENT FUNDS[15]

YEAR	CRORES OF RS. WEST PAK	CRORES OF RS. E. PAK	% OF TOTAL
1950-55	1129	524	32
1955-60	1655	524	24
1960-65	3355	1404	30
1965-70	5195	2141	29
Total	11334	4593	29

The economic exploitation was so severe that the per-capita income of people in East Pakistan was significantly lower than people in West Pakistan. The disparity in the per-capita income continued to widen, and the military dictator did nothing to remedy the disparity.

Although it was one country, but there was a lack of mobility of manpower from East Pakistan to West Pakistan. Economic exploitation did not end there. East Pakistan, which was the largest producer of jute, earned most of the foreign exchange, but West Pakistan got most of the imports.

15 Source: Reports of the advisory panels for the fourth five year plan 1970–75, Vol. 1. Published by the planning commission of Pakistan.

FOREIGN TRADE 1947–67

POSITION	MIL. RS. E. PAK	MIL. RS. W. PAK
Exports	20,982,391	15,704,714
Imports	15,183,796	34,388,211
Balance	5,798,595	-18,683,497

Because of this disparity, there was growing dissention in East Pakistan. The military government continued to suppress this dissent.

EDUCATIONAL DISPARITY

B esides the economic exploitation of East Pakistan, there was a great deal of disparity in education between East and West Pakistan. The population in East Pakistan grew at a faster rate, and therefore the enrolled student population in East Pakistan was higher. In both East and West Pakistan, the majority of the schools were publicly financed. The total national expenditure for education increased from 1 percent of GDP in 1947 to 2.6 percent of GDP in 1964. This growth in expenditures was well matched in growth of schools in West Pakistan. However, there was virtually no growth in East Pakistan. This was because of clear discriminatory policy of the military government.

Development in education is a function of resource allocation by the central government. The number of school-age children in East Pakistan grew at a faster rate than West Pakistan, but it usually received only 20 percent of the educational budget in spite of having 54 percent of the population. Between 1947 and 1971, the school infrastructure steeply declined in East Pakistan. During this period, West Pakistan gained a total of 35,287 additional primary schools, while schools in East Pakistan actually declined by 902. This left classrooms in East Pakistan overcrowded.

From the very birth of Pakistan it seems that all the policies of the central government, which were dominated by West Pakistanis, were discriminatory toward East Pakistan and were against a united and strong Pakistan. Pakistan as a Muslim country would have been much stronger if the two provinces were united. It cannot be said with certainty whether the CIA was dictating the policies of the central government. However, it was certain that US support was always overwhelming for the military dictators in Pakistan. Therefore, it can be said that the CIA, from the very inception of Pakistan, desired Pakistan to remain weak as a Muslim country.

MILITARY DICTATORSHIP 1958–1971

General Mohammad Ayub Khan proclaimed martial law on October 27, 1958, which led to the dismissal of President Iskander Mirza. General Ayub Khan took over as president of Pakistan. General Ayub Khan justified his action by saying the country was headed towards national disintegration. The declaration of martial law brought the army into the forefront of politics. (Ninety percent of the army was from West Pakistan, although they were only 46 percent of Pakistan's population). Therefore, the total administration was dominated by West Pakistani.

General Ayub Khan promised a growth-oriented economy and political stability. However, he was not attentive to the dissatisfaction of the Bengalis and the growing disparity between East and West Pakistan. Soon after General Ayub Khan came to power, there seemed to be overwhelming support for the dictator from the United States. General Ayub Khan enjoyed good relationship with the United States and became a good personal friend of John F. Kennedy.

The elites in Pakistan's politics acknowledged the existence of the economic and political disparity between East and West Pakistan, which continued to widen, and the military dictator did nothing to remedy the situation. The state was the promoter of economic growth, and economic growth was biased in favor of West Pakistan.

Because Bengalis were deprived from being in the ruling class, the position of the Bengalis continued to deteriorate. East Pakistan was the largest producer of jute in the world. After partition, there were no jute-processing facilities in East Pakistan. West Pakistani industrialists came to East Pakistan to establish jute-processing industries. Bengalis were deprived of being industrialists in their own land. The economic gap continued to widen, and General Ayub Khan did nothing to narrow the gap. Bengalis were looked upon as an inferior race, which resulted in the ruling elites oppressing the Bengalis.

General Ayub Khan, in order to legitimize his presidency, started the process called basic democracy. Basic democracy called for the people to elect eighty thousand union members, forty thousand in East Pakistan and forty thousand in West Pakistan. Once these eighty thousand members were elected, the members would then vote for the president. General Ayub Khan was a presidential candidate and the combined opposition party nominated Fatima Jinnah, the sister of Mohammed Ali Jinnah, founder of Pakistan. Although Fatima Jinnah lost the election, she did much better in East Pakistan.

During General Ayub Khan's rule, the Bengali intellectuals became more and more vocal against the economic exploitation and disparity. The Bengali intellectuals made the following three arguments: 1. East Pakistan had become a market for dumping West Pakistani products at a price higher than the prevailing world market price. 2. The foreign trade policy was biased in favor of West-Pakistani interests. 3. The ruling elite allocated and distributed resources in favor of West Pakistan. The study of the political economy of Pakistan clearly reveals the exploitation of East Pakistan by West Pakistan.

The political party of the Bengalis, the Awami League led by Sheikh Mujibur Rahman, was championing the quest for autonomy and came up with a six-point agenda, which was accepted as its program. The program was as follows: 1. A federation based on the Lahore Resolution. 2. A central government that dealt only with defense and foreign affairs. 3. Either two separate currencies for the two wings or same currency for both wings, with a provision that flight of capital is prevented and each wing maintains separate revenue accounts. 4. The units will be given the authority to levy taxes and to collect revenue. 5. There will be separate foreign exchange accounts for both the wings. 6. A paramilitary force will be set up for East Pakistan.

Sheikh Mujibur Rahman was elected as president of the Awami League, and he immediately began a massive campaign in East Pakistan to fulfill these demands. The military regime decided to take an approach of confrontation and put Mujib under detention. Mujib was still an unknown figure in East Pakistan. General Ayub Khan, in an attempt to ruin Mujib's credibility, charged Mujib and some junior Bengali military officers with a conspiracy to secede from Pakistan and create an independent state in East Pakistan with the aid of India. This was known as Agartala Conspiracy case.

The military government of General Ayub Khan failed to prove its case against Mujib. This made Mujib extremely popular in East Pakistan. Bengalis looked upon Mujib as the leader who championed the cause of Bengalis. President Ayub Khan was forced to drop all charges against Mujib. In order to resolve the problem, Ayub Khan invited Mujib to a round-table conference to discuss the political structure of the nation and to set ground work to solve the national problem. The negotiation did not succeed.

The masses in East Pakistan continued their demonstrations on the street for democracy, elections, and economic justice. The government was unable to control the masses in East Pakistan, and this led to the downfall of General Ayub Khan. On March 25, 1969, he handed over power to yet another General Yahya Khan. During Ayub Khan's rule, the government was centralized. The central government was dominated by West Pakistanis. The aspirations of the Bengalis were ruthlessly suppressed. Although there was economic growth, the economic disparity of East and West Pakistan continued to widen.

Bengalis became more militant. The national problem could not be solved with the military in power and lack of democratic power to make changes in policies. General Yahya Khan took power after massive demonstrations and militant actions in East Pakistan. Yahya Khan's regime tried to portray that they were in power for a short time. The regime of General Yahya Khan declared that it wanted to transfer power to the elected representative of the people. Elections were to be held on the basis of popular franchise. According to the legal framework order, the seats of the national assembly would be distributed based on the population of each of the provinces. The allocation of national assembly seats were as follows:

PROVINCES	SEATS
East Pakistan	169
Punjab	85
Sind	28
Baluchistan	5
NWFP	19
Tribal Areas	7
Total	313

There were some objections to the proposed structure and mechanism to transfer power and transition to democracy. However, the Awami League (the political party of East Pakistan), led by Sheikh Mujibur Rahman, decided to participate in the election. The Awami League promised to implement the six-point program. The election was seen as a referendum on autonomy.

Bengalis saw this as an opportunity to have political power for the first time since the creation of Pakistan. This was an opportunity for the Bengalis to get out of economic exploitation and neglect of their aspirations. In the election that followed, the Awami League won a decisive and landslide victory at the national assembly election, with the right to form a government. The results are as follows:

PARTIES	SEATS
Awami League (Mujib)	167
PPP (Z. A. Bhutto)	88
Other parties	44
Independents	14
Total	313

The military, bureaucracy, and businesses, all dominated by West Pakistanis, were shocked at the election results. For the first time in Pakistan's history, they faced the prospect that central government power would go to the Bengalis, and the Awami League would frame the constitution based on six-point program. This would virtually end exploitation of East Pakistan by West Pakistan and stop the transfer of wealth from East Pakistan to West Pakistan.

In West Pakistan, Pakistan People's Party, led by former foreign minister Zulfiqar ali Bhutto, emerged as the dominant party. Bhutto wanted to protect the elites and bureaucrats in West Pakistan. Bhutto declared that he would not allow the constitution to be framed without his consent. Bhutto was opposed to taking the role of opposition and minority party in the national assembly. Negotiation between Bhutto, Mujib, and Yahya Khan continued but failed to resolve the problem. The West Pakistani elite were unwilling to accept Awami League's six-point program and denounced it as a secession plan. While the negotiation with the Awami League was proceeding, the army attacked the Bengalis to crush their demands. The central government transferred army divisions from West Pakistan to East Pakistan. General Yahya Khan dissolved the civilian cabinet and formed a military cabinet.

The military set up a plan known as Operation Searchlight. The objective of the plan was to stop all activities of the Awami League, arresting the maximum number of Bengali intellectuals, students, and political activists, and at the same time disarming the Bengali troops.

SHEIKH MUJIBUR RAHMAN

While Sheikh Mujib continued his dialogue with Yahya Khan, the military buildup in East Pakistan continued. The Awami League and Mujib himself did not predict that the military would strike at the general population. Mujib demanded withdrawal of the troops and handing over power to the elected representative of the people. During this period, there were clashes between the troops and civilians, resulting in many civilian casualties. The radicals and militants within the Awami League called upon Sheikh Mujib to declare independence. On March 7, 1971, Sheikh Mujib, in a very articulate and carefully phrased speech, called upon the people of East Pakistan to resist and confront the military with whatever arms they had. He stopped just short of declaring independence.

The Awami League began a nonviolent noncooperation movement and adopted the following measures: 1. Refusal to pay taxes. 2. Stopping the flight of capital from East Pakistan to West Pakistan. 3. Observation of strikes. 4. Hoisting of black flags. 5. Access to media for the opposition. 6. Setting up council of action under Awami League leadership.

The Awami League was extremely successful, and the administrative control of East Pakistan passed from Pakistani authorities to the Awami League. While the military buildup in East Pakistan continued, General Yahya Khan, along with Bhutto, flew to Dhaka on March 15, 1971, for a discussion with Mujib. The discussion with Mujib was not successful.

The military dictator and Bhutto, along with other officials of the central government, left Dhaka without prior notice on March 25, 1971. Immediately at 11:00 p.m., army movement began, and the Pakistani Army began mass killings of Bengali civilians—men, women, and children, including rape, violence, and looting. It is estimated that just on the night of March 25, 1971, the Pakistani Army killed over one hundred thousand civilian Bengalis, police, and Bengali troops. Mujib declared independence just before he was arrested by the Pakistani Army. However, most of the leaders of the Awami League were able to escape to India, where they set up a provisional government of Bangladesh in exile. In India, with the help of the Indian Army, the Bangladeshi liberation force was created, trained, and sent to Bangladesh to fight the Pakistani Army.

THE BIRTH OF BANGLADESH

After Mujib was arrested on March 25, 1971, he was taken to West Pakistan and put in a jail. The Pakistani Army continued its massive killings, rape, and violence. The provisional government in India organized the Liberation Army, who were trained by Indian Army.

The Bengalis resisted the Pakistani Army with primitive arms and built barricades and created obstacles. The areas and villages where the Pakistani Army could not penetrate were declared liberated zones. Bengali troops defected from the Pakistani Army and initiated the liberation struggle.

The Pakistani Army launched a systematic attack on Bengalis. They shelled the Dhaka University campus, killing teachers and students. They broke into women's dormitories, raping and killing them. The army used machine guns and heavy artillery to crush Bengali civilians, local police, and Bengali troops. Mass graves were used for the dead. After the first night of attack on the Bengalis, the leader of West Pakistan's dominant party, Bhutto, was flown back to West Pakistan. The military attack on the Bengalis made them united. Irrespective of political affiliation, they were willing to fight till the end for self-rule and freedom. Bengalis tried through a peaceful and constitutional process to gain political and economic justice. However, it was clear that West Pakistani military rulers would never allow Bengalis any political power or self-determination through peaceful negotiation.

The Awami League in India established guerilla warfare training camps under the supervision of the Indian Army and retained control over the guerilla movement. Ten million refugees fled to India to escape the killing, brutality, and rape of the Pakistani Army. India was delighted with this opportunity. The Indian Army was extremely helpful. It helped to train the guerillas and supplied them with arms and ammunition to go back to East Pakistan and fight the Pakistani Army. There was overwhelming sympathy for the Bengalis from all over the world. However, the United States continued to support the Pakistani military dictator.

The international situation altered with the signing of Indo-Soviet treaty, which guaranteed the security of India. On December 6, 1971, India officially recognized Bangladesh as a sovereign and independent country. The Bangladesh Liberation Army, along with Indian Army, moved into East Pakistan and was able to overcome the Pakistani Army easily. The Pakistani Army decided to surrender to the joint command of Bangladesh and Indian forces on December 16, 1971. Bangladesh became a free country.

Between March 25, 1971, and December 16, 1971, it is estimated that nearly 3 million Bengalis were killed by the Pakistani Army and raped more than half a million women. Ten million refugees fled to India, but twenty million returned from India. While these atrocities and killings were going on to suppress democracy, the United States and Henry Kissinger continued to support the military dictator of West Pakistan. While all these killings were taking place in East Pakistan, Mujib was kept alive in a West Pakistani prison. After the liberation of Bangladesh, Mujib was released from jail and flown back to Bangladesh. There was a moral obligation to bring the killers and the rapists of 1971 to justice, not only to uphold the dignity of their victims but also to acknowledge the bravery and sacrifice of the Bengalis to achieve freedom. However, Mujib, upon his return from the West Pakistani prison, declared a general amnesty.

Several conclusions can be drawn from the events since the inception of a military dictatorship in Pakistan until the liberation of Bangladesh. Ever since the military dictator General Ayub Khan came to power in 1958, there was overwhelming support from the United States and the CIA. The United States does not want to see a strong Muslim country anywhere in the world. Therefore the United States and the CIA supported the military dictator, and the CIA dictated policies that would cause turmoil within Pakistan, and Pakistan remain a weak nation. US support for Pakistan's military government continued even when democracy was being suppressed and genocide was taking place in East Pakistan.

GENERAL YAHYA KHAN

Photo © Yahya and Nixon.jpg:Yahoo1 at
en.wikipediaderivative work: Vasyatka1
(Yahya and Nixon.jpg) [Public domain],
from Wikimedia Commons

India, which always wanted to see a weaker Pakistan, took advantage
of the situation by helping the Bengalis and the freedom fighters.
During this struggle for liberation, the Soviets took the side of India
and Bangladesh by signing the Indo-Soviet treaty. The United States
wanted Pakistan to break and become weaker. Mujib was kept alive in
a Pakistani prison because he was expected to give general amnesty to
Pakistani Army. It was US policy and support for the Pakistani military dictator that turned Muslims against Muslims. It was Muslims
killing Muslims. It was Muslims raping Muslim women.

Soon after independence on December 16, 1971, the Indian
Army sabotaged and paralyzed the Bangladeshi jute mills, and
Bangladesh's main foreign exchange earnings were stopped. India
wanted the jute mills in Calcutta to capture the world market for jute
products. Mujib returned to Bangladesh on January 10, 1972. His

popularity was at its peak, and no other political party could achieve the broad-based appeal like the Awami League. In March of 1973, Mujib's Awami League won a landslide victory in the parliamentary elections. Mujib gradually began to be more authoritarian.

In 1974 Mujib proclaimed a state of emergency and amended the constitution with the intention to limit the powers of the legislative and judicial branches. He established executive presidency and began a one-party system. Mujib became the president and dissolved all political parties except his own BAKSAL or Bangladesh Krishak Sramik Awami League. All members of the parliament had to join BAKSAL. Mujib's rule was tyrannical; he followed a pro-Indian policy. Bangladesh's economy was stagnant, and widespread corruption made Mujib a very unpopular man in a very short time.

In August 1975, Mujib was assassinated by some mid-level army officers. The government was formed by Khandoker Mustaque, an associate of Mujib's who was also known to have the American connection. However, later in November there were successive military coups, and General Ziaur Rahman emerged successful. In 1978 Ziaur Rahman was elected as president for a five-year term. General Zia allowed opposition political parties to emerge. In February of 1979, Zia's Bangladesh Nationalist Party won the majority in the parliamentary elections. Zia was very popular. However, in 1981 Zia was assassinated by dissident elements within the military. Vice President Justice Abdus Sattar was sworn in as president. He called for elections within six months and was elected president. Justice Abdus Sattar was ineffective as president, and in March 1982 Army Chief of Staff General Ershad took over in a bloodless coup.

Because of General Ershad's policies, the opposition to his rule grew stronger, and there were violent public protests. Dissatisfaction to his rule grew stronger, forcing him to resign in December of 1990.

GENERAL ZIA AND GENERAL ERSHAD

Once Bangladesh had civilian rule, two parties emerged as winners
by turn: the Awami League, led by the daughter of late Mujib, and the
Bangladesh Nationalist Party, led by the wife of late General Ziaur
Rahman. Although Hasina Sheikh and Begum Khaleda Zia were

elected after 1991, the actual government is being run by a handful of Hindu minorities. Although Bangladesh is supposedly 88 percent Muslim, it is being led by a Hindu government installed by the CIA. Because of this, Bangladesh has become a dumping ground for Indian goods. Moreover, there is reason to believe that as much as 30 percent of Bangladesh's population is composed Indians who have come to Bangladesh, even during the military dictatorship of Pakistan, illegally. They are definitely Hindus in private life but Muslims in public life. They did not come for better economic reasons but with political motives. They are better educated and therefore can effectively compete for better public and private sector jobs. Their main purpose is to destroy Bangladesh as a Muslim country and eventually take over Bangladesh's political power. It can be said that the CIA is the mastermind behind this plan. Bangladesh has become impotent as a nation.

PAKISTAN AFTER 1971

After East Pakistan became the free country of Bangladesh, Pakistan
lost its major province and 56 percent of the population. In Pakistan,
Zulfiqar Ali Bhutto became president. However, after amendments
to the constitution, a parliamentary system was adopted in 1973.
The real power was with the prime minister. Zulfiqar Ali Bhutto was
sworn in as the prime minister of Pakistan on August 14, 1973.

ZULFIQAR ALI BHUTTO

Photo © Fototeca online a comunismului
românesc #37402X8X11 (02.05.2013)
Română: Aspecte din timpul vizitei oficiale de
prietenie a președintelui Consiliului de Stat
al României, Nicolae Ceaușescu împreună cu
Elena Ceaușescu în Pakistan.(ianuarie 1973)

Bhutto was in power, and in the 1977 election his Pakistan's Peoples
Party won most of the parliamentary seats. But Bhutto was accused of
rigging the election. Bhutto had an authoritarian style of leadership and
tried to suppress the opposition. He was also viewed by many as being

responsible for the dismemberment of East Pakistan. However, it was Bhutto who started Pakistan's nuclear program. Bhutto's unpopularity allowed General Ziaul Haq to declare martial law in July of 1977. During General Ziaul Haq's presidency, the Russians invaded Afghanistan, and Pakistan provided shelter to millions of Afghan refugees. General Ziaul Haq promised the Islamization of Pakistan, and he helped organize the Afghan resistance to the Soviet invasion. America flooded Pakistan with money to build up the Afghan resistance force.

GENERAL ZIAUL HAQ

Photo by US Government [Public domain], via Wikimedia Commons

General Ziaul Haq swore in Mohammad Khan Junejo as prime minister, but the real power remained with General Ziaul Haq. Mohammad Khan Junejo remained prime minister from 1985 until 1988. General Ziaul Haq, just like any other dictator, was close to America, and he was doing exactly what America was asking Pakistan to do. It was during General Ziaul Haq's presidency that the execution of Zulfiqar Ali Bhutto took place. Zulfiqar Ali Bhutto was greedy for power, but it was he who started Pakistan's nuclear program. He was a true and patriotic Pakistani, but Ziaul Haq killed him. However, General Ziaul Haq died, along with the US ambassador to Pakistan, in a plane crash in August 1988.

After the death of General Ziaul Haq, Benazir Bhutto, daughter of Zulfiqar Ali Bhutto, was sworn in as prime minister—the first woman to govern an Islamic state. Benazir Bhutto faced some problems from opposition, and in November 1988, fresh elections were held. Benazir Bhutto again became the prime minister. After the death of General Ziaul Haq, Ghulam Ishaq Khan became president. Constitutional amendments gave the president significant power. Therefore, the prime minister and the president were in conflict with the appointments of the military chiefs and superior court judges.

The conflict came to a head when, in August 1990, President Ghulam Ishaq Khan dissolved the national assembly and dismissed Benazir Bhutto as prime minister. Elections were held in October 1990, and Muhammad Nawaz Sharif was elected as prime minister. Nawaz Sharif was in power until April of 1993. Fresh elections were held, and Benazir Bhutto returned as prime minister for a second term, and Farooq Ahmed Khan Leghari was elected as the new president of Pakistan. He followed the same tradition of dismissing elected officials by using the eighth amendment of the constitution.

Benazir Bhutto faced problems from the opposition. She made significant progress, but in September 1996, her brother, Mir Murtaza Bhutto, was assassinated under mysterious circumstances. In November 1996, President Farooq Leghari dismissed Benazir Bhutto's government on charges of corruption and mismanagement. President Farooq Leghari visited India in April 1995. Benazir Bhutto's government was dismissed while she was trying to strengthen Pakistan's defense. She came to the United States for the approval of F-16 fighters, for which Pakistan paid but was denied shipment. Benazir Bhutto came to the United States, and the Senate approved the sale of F-16 fighters to Pakistan.

BENAZIR BHUTTO

President Sardar Farooq Leghari dismissed Benazir Bhutto's government in November 1996. After the elections, Nawaz Sharif became
prime minister again in February 1997. Nawaz Sharif faced serious
confrontations with the executive and judiciary branches, which led

to the resignation of President Leghari in December 1997. It was during Nawaz Sharif's tenure that Pakistan carried out its nuclear test in May 1998. Nawaz Sharif was removed from power in October 1999 by General Parvez Musharraf. General Musharraf was born in India but migrated to Pakistan with his family in 1947. He eventually took over as president in 2001. It was Zulfiqar Ali Bhutto who initiated the need for nuclear power after India did nuclear tests in 1974. For Pakistan's security, nuclear weapons were essential to deter India. The United States put lot of pressure on Pakistan and India for a moratorium on nuclear tests. Pakistan agreed to do so if India agreed. Pakistan always wanted a nuclear-free zone, but India developed nuclear weapons first. America lifted all sanctions against India, but the sanctions are still in place for Pakistan.

Pakistan and India have been at odds over the Indian occupation of Kashmir. The people of Kashmir are more than 80 percent Muslim, and they want to be liberated from India. There was a UN Security Council resolution on August 13, 1948, that calls for the people of Kashmir to determine their fate in a plebiscite supervised by the UN. India never allowed the people of Kashmir to vote in a plebiscite. The people of Kashmir are brutally suppressed by the Indian Army, and the world keeps watching. The freedom fighters of Kashmir continue to struggle, but no one will help the Muslims of Kashmir except Pakistan. Pakistan only gives moral, diplomatic, and political support to the freedom fighters of Kashmir. The United States and Bill Clinton always warned Pakistan not to go to war with India over Kashmir. After General Parvez Musharraf came to power, he was very cordial with India but could not solve Kashmir's problems. General Parvez Musharraf forgot the Muslims of Kashmir and normalized relations with India.

NAWAZ SHARIF AND GENERAL PARVEZ MUSHARRAF

Photo © Saqib Qayyum / CC-BY-SA-2.0

INDONESIA

Before I start to discuss the political and economic events in Indonesia, I would like to remind the readers that the United States, the superpower of the world, wants to suppress and cripple the Muslims by depriving them of good education and technology. The CIA has penetrated in every Muslim country and has allowed the Indians to penetrate every Muslim country to suppress the Muslims. There were many visits by several Indian prime ministers to Indonesia, and General Suharto of Indonesia visited India several times. There are about five million Hindus in Indonesia, and about fifty thousand nonresident Indians live in Indonesia. The governments in all Muslim countries are powerless and must do what the CIA wants. The CIA uses Indians to penetrate into every Muslim country to destroy that society.

Photo © World Economic Forum / CC-BY-SA-2.0

It was Sukarno who unified all the islands and fought the Japanese and later Dutch occupation for a free Indonesia. On December 27, 1949, the Dutch formally transferred sovereignty, and Indonesia became a free country. This was the birth of the largest Muslim country. On December 28, 1949, Sukarno returned from Dutch prison to lead free Indonesia. Today Indonesia has a population of 224 million. In 1950 Indonesia was formally admitted to the United Nations.

Soon after independence, Indonesia adopted a parliamentary form of government, where the parliament chooses the president. Nationwide elections took place in 1955, but Indonesia failed to install a stable government. The role of Islam in Indonesian politics was uncertain because Sukarno was in favor of a secular state. However, even before the election, Indonesia and India signed a treaty of friendship. Indonesia's beginning was not peaceful at all. In 1951 there was a rebellion led by a colonel in South Sulawese, and at the same time there were strikes and demonstrations, which led to the arrests of over fifteen thousand PKI members in Medan and Jakarta.

The United States was very supportive and in 1952 provided military aid, thereby establishing a good relationship with the Indonesian Army. However, there was a question raised about accepting such military aid, and Sukarno's cabinet was dissolved. In 1953 Sukarno made it clear in a speech that Indonesia will remain a secular state and accommodate both Muslims and non-Muslims. During the same year, Indonesia established diplomatic relations with China. Once again in June, Prime Minister Wilopo resigned and was succeeded by Ali Sastromidjojo. Soon after there was rebellion against the central government in Aceh, and East Timor became a province of Portugal. In 1954 Sukarno banned military officers from campaigning in uniform.

In April of 1955, Sukarno participated in Asia-Africa conference where it began the Non-Align Movement. During this meeting,

Indonesia and China signed an agreement that allowed dual citizenship to Chinese living in Indonesia. In 1956 Sukarno was concerned over military commanders who were building power bases in their districts. He decided to send them overseas on diplomatic missions. Prime Minister Ali Sastromidjojo followed policies of Indonesian nationalism, but it increased corruption and inflation, which made it unfavorable for investment.

SUKARNO

Photo © User *drew on en.wikipedia [Public domain], via Wikimedia Commons

In May of 1956, Sukarno visited the United States. In October while he was on a visit to the Soviet Union and China, there was an attempted coup, and the following month there was another coup attempt. There was a great deal of dissention within the army. Several army officers signed a manifesto expressing their dissatisfaction with the central government in Jakarta. A colonel seized power in Padang, and another colonel seized power in Medan. General Suharto became commander in central Java. Colonel Sumual took control of all government functions in Eastern Indonesia and demanded more powers for Sukarno and less power for the assembly and the cabinet. In June some army officers rebelled and declared North Sulewese autonomous state. Sukarno in a speech proposed guided democracy in an attempt to unify. Guided democracy includes members of all political parties and allowed Sukarno to consolidate power. Sukarno nationalized all Dutch businesses, which hurt the economy because civil servants and military officers who ran the businesses became corrupt.

In 1957 General Nasution went to the United States to ask for a loan and military aid, but he was turned down. However, General Nasution later received aid in 1958 from both the Soviet Union and the United States. Ever since Sukarno came to power, there was some form of unrest. In July of 1957, there was a grenade attack on PKI offices in Jakarta. There was a grenade attack on Sukarno himself, killing six people. Sukarno had to share his power with the military. General Nasution demanded a dual role for the military, a military force, and an organization for social development. In February of 1958, there was a rebellion against the government in Bukittinge, and the United States promised to aid the rebels. However, Sukarno responded with force, and the air force bombed Padang, Bukittinge and Manado. Army soldiers were deployed and landed in Sumatra, taking over Medan. A US pilot was shot down while helping the rebels. Both Padang and Bukittinge came under the central government.

Sukarno dissolved the cabinets and parliament and restored the 1945 constitution. The new parliament would have 575 members, mostly selected by Sukarno. Sukarno allowed the formation of Parisada Dharma to advance the interest of the Hindu community. In October of 1959, General Nasution dismissed General Suharto, who was accused of corruption and demanding money from different businesses in Java. However, General Suharto was reinstated to the military staff college in Bandung. In 1960 Indonesia began to receive Soviet military aid, and Kruschev visited Jakarta. In March of 1960, the elected assembly (DPR) rejected Sukarno's budget. Sukarno dissolved the assembly and eventually replaced it with an assembly whose members were chosen by Sukarno and included military officers. The Muslim groups, along with some military, formed a group that was anti-communist. Sukarno banned this party.

General Nasution visited both Washington and Moscow for military aid. Sukarno maintained good relations with the Soviet Union and the United States. In 1961 Indonesia received military aid from the Soviet Union; similar aid was declined by Washington. In March of 1961, KOSTRAD, a special force, was formed, and General Suharto was appointed commander of that unit. In April Sukarno visited the United States and met President Kennedy. Soon after, with US support, work began on a nuclear research facility at Bandung. At that time, Muslim rebels in Sumatra and Java began to surrender. During the same year, Sukarno signed a treaty of friendship and cooperation with China. In January of 1962, there was an assassination attempt on Sukarno. However, soon after Sukarno mobilized the army to take over West Iran by force from the Dutch. The United States was aiding the Dutch by allowing Dutch flights to refuel in Alaska. The US embassy in Jakarta was attacked in retaliation, forcing the United States not to allow any Dutch flight to refuel in Alaska. Later the Dutch were willing to negotiate with Indonesia. In April of 1962, Hinduism earned recognition as an official religion. The Islamic movement led by Darul Islam fell apart with the execution of its leader, Kartosuvirgo. In September the United Nations ratified the West Iran agreement.

In 1963 Sukarno tightened its control over publishers, requiring them to submit a copy everything published within forty-eight hours of publication. Sukarno publicly opposed the creation of Malaysia. Later the president of the Philippines called for a conference for a possible federation of Philippines, Indonesia, and Malaysia. It was not fruitful. But an accord was reached to continue discussion.

Indonesia was facing numerous problems. Sukarno had to cut the budget, increased prices, and devalued the rupiah in order to convince the IMF to give Indonesia aid. Malaysia finally became free after Britain signed the final agreement. This made Sukarno very unhappy. Sukarno nationalized British properties in Indonesia, and

Kennedy cut off all military aid to Indonesia. US President Johnson stopped economic aid to Indonesia. There was a confrontation between Indonesian troops and Malaysian troops. The British and the United States aided the Malaysians.

Finally in 1964 a ceasefire was arranged by Robert Kennedy of the United States. By this time, the Indonesian economy was in shambles. There were shortages of food and clothing. Prices increased by more than 700 percent. Besides these domestic problems, Indonesia continued to raid Malaysia. It was Muslims fighting Muslims. A UN resolution was passed to condemn Indonesia, but it was vetoed by the Soviet Union.

In April of 1965, Sukarno nationalized all foreign enterprises. By the end of 1965, violence broke out, and the army was rounding up communists. Islamic groups were fighting the communists, and more than two hundred and fifty thousand people died in this violence. The US Consulate was barricaded, and the Indian embassy was burned by a mob. Sukarno faced many problems, including ill health, and prices were increasing by 50 percent per week.

In a speech, Sukarno reaffirmed his anti-imperialist policy. There was massive unrest throughout Indonesia. Rebel soldiers took over Merdika Square in front of the Presidential Palace in Jakarta on September 30, 1965. On October 1, 1965, General Suharto took over as army chief of staff and promised to protect Sukarno. In a radio speech, he said he was pro-Sukarno, anti-United States, and anti-CIA.

Sukarno's fifteen years of rule were marked by constant turmoil and unstable cabinets. During his rule, there were several rebellions, and Indonesia faced external threats from the Dutch. The economy was stagnant; there were shortages of rice, a staple food, and there was rapid inflation. Sukarno was a patriotic leader but could not accomplish anything of significance during his rule. He was a popular leader but was not listening to the dictates of the CIA 100 percent.

Toward the end of his rule in 1965, inflation was over 700 percent. There was massive violence, and several hundred thousand people died. In January 1966, Sukarno wanted to nationalize US oil companies' properties, but General Suharto opposed him. Sukarno was under pressure and signed a document giving broad powers to Suharto. Later in March, General Suharto arrested Sukarno and his cabinet. After that Sukarno lived under house arrest till his death in 1970.

In March 1966, General Suharto took over with clandestine support from the CIA. After Suharto took over, Indonesia formally ended its confrontation with Malaysia. In January of 1967, General Suharto guaranteed that no further properties would be nationalized. He offered a tax holiday and allowed foreign companies to send their profits overseas, and he returned all British and US properties. After this, the United States and Japan were quick to pledge significant aid to Indonesia.

In March of 1967, General Suharto was named acting president. Suharto broke diplomatic relations with China and closed all Chinese-language newspapers and schools. To reduce the influence of communists, Suharto required every citizen to register his or her religion either as Islam, Hindu, Buddhist, Catholic, or Protestant. This caused a significant growth in the number of Catholics and Protestants. In late '60s and '70s, Suharto introduced a new concept of Kebatinun as another religion. This was in an attempt to reduce Islam and its influence on Indonesian politics. Even after all these, Muslims accounted for 90 percent of the population. In September 1968, the World Bank approved its first loan to Indonesia. Suharto soon began to misuse his power. He granted a clove import monopoly to his half-brother. Mrs. Suharto was granted a monopoly on the import, milling, and distribution of flour and wheat.

GENERAL SUHARTO

Photo By the Government of Republic of Indonesia
[Public domain], via Wikimedia Commons

President Nixon visited Jakarta in July 1969, followed by General Suharto's visit to the United States in January 1970. Around 60 percent of Suharto's first five-year plan's government budget was met with foreign aid. Suharto banned government employees from any political activity. However, there was widespread corruption, and in August of 1970 Suharto closed the anticorruption commission.

Suharto allowed elections to take place in 1971. There were restrictions on all political parties' activities except Golkar. The military supported Golkar. The military screened all candidates, and candidates from many parties were not cleared by the military and could not run for election. Therefore, in the election Golkar won two-thirds of the seats in the assembly. The new assembly had a total of 460 members, of which 207 were chosen by General Suharto, 123 were chosen by political parties, and 130 were chosen by provinces. Suharto picked most of his choices from the army.

After 1973 and until the end of Suharto presidency in 1998, only three political parties were allowed: Golkar, which was backed by the government and the military; PPP, which represented the interests of the Muslims; and the PDI, formed by Sukarno's supporters and a Christian alliance. However, only Golkar was allowed to campaign freely and outside the city limits. Other parties were not allowed to campaign outside the city limits. All government employees and school teachers had to vote for Golkar.

During 1974 there were rice shortages. This was followed by student demonstrations and protests. Riots broke out, and there were widespread arrests. Public meetings were banned, and many newspapers and magazines were shut down. Pertamina, the Indonesian oil company, was heavily in debt because of widespread corruption and mismanagement. Pertimina defaulted on many debts, and later the Bank of Indonesia agreed to pay its debt.

There was violence in East Timor, the military entered, and casualties were as high as two hundred thousand. Over ten thousand troops were either killed or wounded. Indonesia eventually took control of East Timor and installed a government. In 1976 East Timor officially became a province of Indonesia. In 1978, Suharto was elected by his handpicked assembly for a third term. He asked the military to protect their seats in the assembly, even by force if necessary. Suharto became a very corrupt leader. In the late '70s and early '80s, oil revenue continued to flow into Indonesia, bur foreign investment was down because of many restrictions and heavy government subsidies for state-owned companies.

In 1982 Suharto banned the wearing of hijabs (a scarf for Muslim women to cover their heads). Nearly a million people turned out for the PPP rally in Jakarta. They got into clash with Golkar, and troops then opened fire on the PPP supporters. Suharto was known for his brutality. He executed several thousand without trial. In spite of all this and public outcry, Suharto was elected by the assembly for a fourth term.

Suharto was well known for favoritism and nepotism. His son was in charge of Sukarno-Hatta International Airport's construction and pocketed about $78 million in cost over-runs. In September of 1984, the army opened fire on a public demonstration, killing sixty-three people. The head of the army was General Bonny Moerdani, a Christian. The rally was for a more free and equitable society and was called together by moderate Islamic politicians.

The assembly elected Suharto again for a fifth term. Suharto and his family pocketed a lot of money, but Indonesia's economic growth began to increase because of economic liberalization. Suharto's rule was marked by repression. In 1990, *International Herald Tribune* and the Asian *Wall Street Journal* were banned from distribution in Indonesia because they printed an article on the business enterprise of the Suharto family. In December of the same year, cigarette manufacturers were required to buy cloves from a company owned by Suharto's son, Tommy Suharto, thereby giving a monopoly to his son. Telecommunication was privatized, and a license was issued to Satelindo, a company owned by Suharto's son Bambang Trihatmodjo. Tommy Suharto founded the Garo supermarket chain with a loan of $100 million from Bank Buni Daya.

The later years of Suharto's presidency were marked by massive demonstrations by students who were rioting in several provinces. Suharto hung onto power until 1998, with repression, brutality, total disregard for human rights, and the CIA's aid. There were massive student demonstrations against Suharto. In a clash between students and Suharto's troops, more than five hundred were killed. Most of the cabinet members resigned after this, and on May 21, 1998, Suharto resigned and B. J. Habibie became the new president. But protests and violence continued, demanding the resignation of Habibie because he was a close associate of Suharto. There were clashes between the army and the demonstrators, and many were killed.

Habibie announced that an election would be held in June 1999. The looting and rioting situation was so bad that General Wiranto ordered his troops to shoot on sight. At the same time, East Timor, which was mostly Christian, wanted to secede from Indonesia and form an independent state. There were many clashes and violence on this issue, and finally Habibie declared that East Timor would become independent by January 2000.

Megawati Sukarnopoutri, the daughter of Sukarno, began to campaign for president. Violence in East Timor continued, and the UN set a date for a plebiscite in East Timor to vote for either autonomy or independence. While the campaigns for election continued, eight Islamic parties signed an agreement to pool votes. On September 1999, the results of the referendum in East Timor were announced, and 78 percent voted for East Timor's independence. There was violence in East Timor between pro-independence and pro Indonesia forces.

In Indonesia, Abdul Rahman Wahid was elected as president and Megawati Sukarnopoutri as vice president. After East Timor gained independence, Aceh began a movement for independence. Riots broke out between Christians and Muslims in Buru and Maluku, and several hundreds were killed. Many of Indonesian islands were pressing for independence, including Irian Jaya. Indonesia faced constant battles to keep its islands united. There was an illegal shipment of arms from overseas that added fuel to this violence.

Violence continued throughout Indonesia. President Wahid put former President Suharto under house arrest. Many of Suharto's corruption charges never made it to court because of Suharto's ill health. In July of 2000, the Indonesian Navy seized a ship loaded with small arms and headed for Maluku. Foreign powers were involved in trying to destabilize the government of Wahid; it couldn't have been anyone else but the CIA. However, because of public pressure, in August former President Suharto was officially charged with corruption. However, the judge dismissed all charges because Suharto was too ill to testify himself.

After Suharto's departure in 1998, Indonesia was in constant turmoil. There were riots and movements for independence, bombing of the Jakarta stock exchange, bombing in many churches, and Muslim-Christian riots. The government of Wahid was unable to control things. In July of 2001, Wahid stepped down, and Megawati Sukarnopoutri became the fifth president of Indonesia.

The CIA is very active in every Muslim country. Their intention is to deprive the Muslims of any progress, development, and technology. After Sukarnopoutri became president and appointed her cabinet, violence in Aceh continued when four banks were bombed and over sixty schools were burnt. Sukarnopoutri faced opposition from Muslim fundamentalists. In September of 2001, President Sukarnopoutri visited Washington and was assured of $150 million in aid and agreed to restore military ties, which were previously broken.

Anti-American sentiments were very much alive in Jakarta, and there were demonstrations in front of the US Embassy. The mob threatened to kill the US ambassador. The CIA's agent, General Suharto, who ruled Indonesia for thirty-three years, was never convicted of any corruption. However, his son Tommy Suharto was charged with corruption and sent to jail. In the meantime, President Sukarnopoutri and Vice President Hamzah Haz both were critical of US actions in Afghanistan while domestic violence continued around Poso and Sulawesi Tenga. There were confrontations between Christians and Muslims. More than one thousand were killed. Later leaders of Muslim and Christian community agreed to end violence and inter-communal fighting.

Indonesia was constantly fighting terrorism because bombing

was a frequent occurrence, and several Muslim groups were accused of such bombings and terrorism. One such incident led investigators to the house of General Santos, where they found over a ton of explosives. General Santos was tried and convicted. In May of 2001, Malaysia, Indonesia, and the Philippines signed an agreement to jointly fight terrorism. Later some terrorists were arrested who confessed having links to the Al-Qaeda. The Australian prime minister tried to change the UN charter to where a country could be attacked if suspected of terrorist activity. Several Muslim countries opposed it.

The question is why the United States, the mightiest nation on earth, with all its intelligence ability could not find and fight Osama bin Laden. Although they ultimately found Osama bin Laden, who was unarmed, they didn't capture him alive because in my opinion they feared that a bit of truth might come out that he was working for the CIA. I have reason to believe that Osama bin Laden is a creation of the CIA to give bad reputation to the Muslims, and the CIA is behind every terrorist attack. The CIA creates terrorism so it can use it as an excuse to invade Muslim countries. The CIA is directly involved in all violence in Indonesia. This is their way of keeping the largest Muslim country unstable and depriving the people of Indonesia progress, stability, and technology. In September 2004, General Bambang Yadhoyono was elected president. Throughout Indonesia's history, the military had a prominent role in politics. Many cabinet members had military backgrounds, and many parliament members had military backgrounds.

MIDDLE EAST

merican history reveals its fondness for slavery. The Middle East has been transformed into American slave states. In order to enslave the Middle East, the British and the United States created the state of Israel in Palestine. This is evident from the Balfour declaration of 1917, which says:

> His Majesty's government view with favor the establishment in Palestine of a national home for the Jewish people, and will use their best endeavors to facilitate the achievement of this object.

The people of Palestine were thrown out of their own land to create the Jewish state of Israel. This permanently created a threat for the entire Middle East. It is this threat that compels every Middle Eastern country to abide by American instruction.

EGYPT

Egypt is the most populous country in the Middle East, with a population of over 77 million, of which 90 percent are Muslims and 10 percent Christians. Egypt is also the home of one of the major centers for Islamic learning, Al-Azhar University, which is about one thousand years old. The British occupied Egypt in 1882 and made it part of the British Empire. Because of growing nationalism, the British declared Egypt independence in 1922, but British influence was an ever-present factor.

However, Egypt's true independence was achieved when Col. Yamal Abdel Nasser overthrew King Farouk in 1952. In 1953, Egypt became a republic. Nasser emerged as a charismatic leader, not only for Egypt but for the entire Arab world. Nasser led the Non-Aligned Movement and granted voting rights to women. He nationalized the Suez Canal, which eventually led to Britain, France, and Israel's invasion of Egypt. Nasser's foreign and military policy was to establish a strong Egypt militarily and economically.

To dampen Nasser's popularity and policies, in 1967 Israel attacked Egypt and virtually destroyed Egypt's armed forces and Israeli occupation of the Sinai Peninsula, the Gaza Strip, the West Bank, and the Golan Heights region. Nasser's popularity nevertheless was still high.

In 1970, Nasser died of a heart attack. After Nasser's death, another army officer, Anwar el Sadat, was elected president. In 1971 Sadat signed a treaty with the Soviet Union, but one year later he asked all Soviet advisors to leave Egypt. Sadat was a devout Muslim and also a charismatic leader. He attacked Israel in October of 1973 to regain occupied territory. However, Sadat did not succeed because the US supply of military weapons to Israel turned the war in Israel's favor.

Sadat's biggest mistake was attacking Israel. He had nowhere to turn for help. He threw the Soviets out of Egypt, and then Sadat became a pawn for America. Sadat became a popular hero in the Arab world, and America did not like that. Whatever Sadat did after the war was not at his own will. The CIA forced Sadat to take a trip to Israel in a quest for peace. This made Sadat very unpopular in the Arab world very quickly, and Egypt was expelled from the Arab league. A Muslim in his right mind would have never gone to Israel for peace.

In 1981, Sadat was assassinated by Muslim fundamentalists—or was it the CIA that was behind the assassination? After Sadat's assassination, Hosni Mubarak took over as president of Egypt. Mubarak was living up to the Camp David Accord signed by Sadat. Israel and Egypt exchanged ambassadors. Mubarak was in compliance with every instruction from the United States. The Muslim brotherhood, which was formed in 1928, remained banned as a political party in Egypt. In Egypt, the president's term is for six years, and since 1981, Mubarak has been reelected for four terms. The president has absolute power in the executive branch. Mubarak's presidency has seen few problems in Egypt, and the opposition party has been unable to defeat him in any of the elections.

Egypt has the largest army in the Middle East except Israel. The armed forces were strengthened with equipment from United States, France, Italy, Britain, and China. Egypt has become strong militarily with equipment such as F-4 jet fighters, F-16 jet fighters, armored personnel carriers, Apache helicopters, antiaircraft missile batteries, etc. But Egypt's forces are no match for Israel's. The United States will never allow Egypt to have a strategic and military advantage over Israel.

One thing needs to be mentioned here—in July of 1954, Israeli spies entered Egypt to sabotage and destroy US property so it could be blamed on Muslim fundamentalists. The plan did not succeed, and the Israeli spies were caught. The prime minister of Israel denied having any knowledge about this plan. This is known as the Lavon Affair. Pinhas Lavon was the defense minister of Israel. In May of 1964, the Palestinian Liberation Organization was formed, with Yasser Arafat as its leader. King Hussein of Jordan was concerned about the power of PLO and its intention to destroy Israel. He almost forced the Palestinians to leave Jordan. The Palestinians sought refuge in Lebanon. In September 1982, Israeli troops and the Lebanese Christian Phalange entered the Palestinian refugee camps of Slera and Shatilla and massacred more than eight hundred unarmed Palestinian refugees.

SAUDI ARABIA

S audi Arabia is the largest country in the Arabian Peninsula. It has a population of 26.7 million, of which 7 million are foreign nationals. These 7 million are mostly from India, Pakistan, Bangladesh, Indonesia, and the Philippines. Saudi Arabia is a monarchy, and the king is the chief executive. The king's authority is supreme. Basically the country is run by the royal family and Sharia law (based on the Quran and its interpretation). The judges are appointed by the king.

Saudi Arabia has a long-standing relationship with the United States. A military training mission was established by the United States in Dahran in 1953. Saudi Arabia's largest trading partners are the United States, Japan, South Korea, and Western Europe. Saudi Arabian forces did not participate in the Six-Day Arab-Israeli War of 1967. Because of Saudi oil revenue, it plays a pivotal role in the Arab world's politics and international affairs.

When Iraq invaded Kuwait, Saddam Hussein had the green signal from the United States, so immediately the United States turned around and deployed forces in Saudi Arabia to liberate Kuwait. However, Saudi Arabia did not allow the United States to use its bases while invading Afghanistan. The Saudis reimbursed the United States with billions of dollars for US troops. The headquarters of the organization of the Islamic Conference is in Jeddah. It is also the headquarters of the Islamic Development Bank.

Saudi Arabia also played a major role in ending the Iran-Iraq War in August of 1988. In March of 2002, Saudi Arabia brought a peace proposal whereby the Arab countries would normalize relations with Israel in exchange for Israel withdrawing from all occupied territories and establishing a Palestinian state with Jerusalem as its capital.

It is apparent that Saudi Arabia has been a loyal partner of the United States ever since the royal family began ruling. However, all that changed after September 11, 2001. Out of the nineteen suicide bombers, fifteen were Saudis. These fifteen were brainwashed to commit this crime. The strangest thing is all fifteen entered the United States and obtained training to commit the suicide attack on the World Trade Center, and neither the CIA nor the FBI knew anything about it. I would have to be a fool to believe that. I want the American people to find out how many Jews were present in the buildings of the World Trade Center on the day of the September 2011 attacks. In May of 2003, suicide bombers killed thirty-five, including nine Americans, in Riyadh, Saudi Arabia. Saudi Arabia has always been America's puppet because it depends on the United States to provide security and stability for the king.

In Saudi Arabia, women are not allowed to drive or to study engineering, law, or journalism. All this gives Islam a bad name. The people of Saudi Arabia are not allowed to change their government. Protests and demonstrations are prohibited. There is no freedom of speech. In Saudi Arabia, Shiite Muslims are discriminated against. Saudi Arabia is trying to create rift between Shiite Muslims and Sunni Muslims. This is exactly what the United States and the West desires. The United States and the West want to divide the Shiite and Sunnis. This is going on for a long time. The British have been playing this game for a long time—the policy of divide and rule.

One Shiite Muslim was sentenced to seven years in prison for talking to a Western journalist about discrimination of Shiite Muslims. In Saudi Arabia, there are about 7 million foreigners. Of those the majority are Indian Hindus who have the best jobs, and they run the technology.

IRAQ

Baghdad was merely a small village until AD 762, when the rulers of the Affasid Caliphate decided to make Baghdad its capital. Baghdad became the center for Muslim scholars and educators, and the ninth century was the golden age of Muslim culture. The stories of the Arabian nights, Aladdin, Ali Baba, and Sinbad the sailor were all written during this period.

Saladin, the legendary Muslim general who defeated the crusaders in the twelfth century, was born in Iraq. Between 1538 and 1914, Iraq was under Ottoman rule. During World War I, the Ottoman Empire fell apart, and the British took control of Iraq. During British rule, they created a division among the Kurds, Sunni, and Shia Muslims because the British policy has always been to divide and rule.

In spite of this, there was rebellion against British imperial power, and in 1900 Churchill agreed to use aerial bombing, chemical weapons, and poison gas on Iraqi civilians. In August of 1921, the British crowned King Faisal, a Saudi, as king of Iraq. In 1932, Iraq became an independent country but remained under British influence. In the early '50s, synagogues were bombed, and later the Zionists did it themselves. Iraq truly became free from British influence when the monarchy was overthrown and Faisal II was executed in 1958. The coup was led by Brig. Abdal Karim Qasim, who became the prime minister and declared Iraq a republic. Qasim quickly took Iraq to the Soviet Bloc and was receiving weapons and arms from the Soviet

Union. In 1959, Saddam Hussein played a leading role in an attempt to assassinate Qasim. The attempt failed. Saddam Hussein had to leave Iraq until 1963 and lived in Egypt and Syria.

Saddam Hussein enrolled in law school in Cairo and was a frequent visitor to the US Embassy in Cairo. In 1963 the CIA and Saddam's Ba'thist Party killed Qasim. The CIA played a major role by constantly staying in touch with military officers and guided the coup. After the coup, Saddam Hussein returned to Iraq. However, soon after the Ba'thist party was overthrown and Saddam Hussein was arrested and put in a minimum-security prison with excellent living conditions.

In 1968, the Ba'thist Party came to power in a coup. Hasan al Bakr became president, and Saddam Hussein became vice president. In 1972, Bakr signed a fifteen-year treaty of friendship between Iraq and the Soviet Union. During the same year, he nationalized the Iraq Petroleum Company. In the meantime, Saddam Hussein as vice president eliminated all rivals by means of torture, confessions, executions, and assassinations.

In 1975 Iran and Iraq signed an agreement ending their border dispute. In 1974, the Kurdish leader felt deprived by the Ba'thist Party for Kurdish autonomy. Conflict between the Kurds and Iraqi forces began. The shah of Iran provided arms to the Kurds, and so did Israel. The CIA was actively helping the Kurdish rebels with arms and military intelligence. In July of 1979, President Bakr resigned and was succeeded by the CIA's main ally in the Ba'thist Party—Saddam Hussein.

During the same year, the Carter administration placed Iraq among countries that sponsor terrorism. US and British policy has always been to create unstable conditions in all Muslim countries and not to allow them to make progress. The CIA's role in putting Saddam Hussein in power was aimed at achieving that objective. Iraq had a bright future before Saddam came into power. The United States was interested in countering the Iranian revolution. The CIA lost Iran, so Saddam came to power with the aid of the CIA and in 1980 attacked Iran. The war continued for eight years, and the United States and Britain were really happy to see two Muslim countries fighting each other and draining their resources. Because of this war, both Iran and Iraq spent billions and incurred massive debt.

Saddam Hussein was a ruthless, brutal ruler who tortured and executed many of his opponents. In 1981, Israel attacked an Iraqi nuclear research center. The war with Iran continued until 1988. The United States armed Saddam. The United States helped Iraq with the production of chemical weapons. Until 1989, the United States supplied biological pathogens for use in warheads. France and Britain also supplied arms to Iraq to strike at Iran. In late December of 1983, Saddam met with Donald Rumsfeld, and the United States supplied Iraq with mustard gas and nerve agent bombs to be used against Iran. Before invading Kuwait, the United States provided Saddam with intelligence and cluster bombs, enabled Iraq's ability in chemical and biological technology, and gave Saddam the green light to attack Kuwait.

Biological agents were regularly shipped by US corporations to Iraq beginning with Ronald Reagan and continuing during George H.W. Bush's approval as head of the CIA and later as vice president under Reagan.

In August 1990, Iraq invaded Kuwait with US approval. However, immediately, the United States became the liberator of Kuwait with the Gulf War. Saddam Hussein continued his presidency of Iraq until he was removed by a US-led coalition in March of 2003.

JORDAN

Jordan became independent from British rule in 1946 and became the Hashemite Kingdom of Jordan. Abdullah was the first king of Jordan. Palestinians assassinated him in 1951. After a short transition rule by Talal, Hussein became king in 1952. After that, Hussein followed a pro-Western policy. Jordan signed a mutual defense pact with Egypt in May of 1967. There are about one million Palestinians who live in Jordan. During the 1973 Arab-Israeli War, no conflict occurred along the Jordan and Israeli border. Hussein signed a peace treaty with Israel, and after Hussein's death in 1999, his son King Abdullah reaffirmed Jordan's peace treaty with Israel. Because Jordan has maintained good relations with the United States for four decades, since 1952 Jordan has received more than 9 billion in US aid and grants. Jordan remained a very peaceful country until the December 2005 bombing in Amman. Jordan proves that it pays to listen to the CIA and maintain good relations with the United States. Jordan only has a population of a little over 5 million.

SYRIA

S yria became independent in 1946. Following its independence, Syria had very volatile political conditions. Between 1946 and 1956, Syria had twenty different cabinets. Between 1956 and 1970, there were many coups and counter-coups.

In 1958, Syria and Egypt merged to form the United Arab Republic. However, the union did not last long. In September 1961, Syria seceded and re-established itself as the Syrian Arab Republic. Syria has a population of over 18 million, of which only 12 percent are Alawis. In 1970 Habiz Al Asad became president and was an Alawite. In the late '70s, there were was upheaval by Sunni Muslims who objected to the rule of the Alawis, who are considered heretical. There was also an uprising by the Muslim Brotherhood. The uprising was brutally crushed by President Asad leveling parts of the city of Hama and killing many thousands.

Syria participated in the US-led multinational coalition against Saddam Hussein in 1990. Syria also participated in the Middle East Peace Conference in Madrid and had face to face negotiations with Israel. Israel occupied the Golan Heights from Syria and still continues to occupy them. During Assad's presidency, Syria was aligned with the Soviet Union and got most of its military equipment from the Soviets. After the death of Hafiz Al Asad, his son, Bashar-Al-Asad, became president in July 2000. After September 11, 2001, Syria cooperated with the United States for countering terrorism. However, Syria opposed the Iraq War in 2003, which caused US-

Syria relations to deteriorate. The United States imposed sanctions against Syria, and imposition of sanctions affected the people of Syria. Assad and his son have been presidents of Syria since 1970. It is difficult to believe they could be in power for such a long time without the blessing of the CIA. It seems consistent with the US policy of having minority governments in Muslim countries.

LIBYA

L ibya became a free and independent country on December 24, 1951. It has a population of over 5 million. Libya proclaimed a constitutional monarchy under King Idris. The discovery of oil in 1959 turned Libya from a poor country to a wealthy country. On September 1, 1969, a military coup led by Colonel Muammar Qaddafi took power, dethroning King Idris. Although no direct link has been found, whether the CIA had any role in this coup is not known. However, subsequent review of the facts will reveal that Qaddafi had links with the CIA.

When Qaddafi took power, he was only twenty-eight years old. In 1970, Qaddafi closed a British military installation near Tripoli and expelled many thousands of Italian residents. Libya became closer to the Soviet Union. US facilities in Libya were also closed. In 1972, Libya and the USSR signed a cooperation treaty. In 1973, Israel shot down a Libyan Airlines jet, killing 108 people on board. In 1977, Libya suspended all diplomatic relations with Egypt. In 1978 a spiritual Shiite Muslim leader from Lebanon disappeared while visiting Libya and was never found. In 1979, Libyans were overjoyed with the success of the Iranian revolution, and a mob ransacked the US embassy in Tripoli. In 1980, Bill Carter, brother of President Jimmy Carter, admitted accepting bribes from Libya. In 1981, all Libyan diplomats were ordered to leave the United States.

It is true that ever since Qaddafi came to power, he has sponsored terrorism, giving a bad name to not only Libya but the entire

Muslim world. In 1982, President Reagan imposed economic sanctions against Libya. In 1983 Edwin Wilson was convicted of supplying arms to Libya. The conviction was later overturned because Wilson worked for the CIA. This was the link that the CIA is always in touch with Qaddafi of Libya and Qaddafi was following CIA instructions.

In 1986, a Berlin nightclub was bombed, and Libya was implicated, and in 2004 Libya agreed to pay $35 million in compensation. In response to this, US warplanes bombed targets in Libya. Qaddafi was supposed to be the target, but US intelligence was so poor that they could not find Qaddafi. (Are we expected to believe that?) Instead they killed many innocent civilians, including Qaddafi's stepdaughter. In 1988, Libya took responsibility for the Pan Am Flight 103 and agreed to pay compensation to the victims. In 1989 a French DC-10 was bombed over the Sahara Desert. Libya was implicated and agreed to pay $170 million in compensation. In 1996, Louis Farrakhan visited Libya and received a pledge of $1 billion from Qaddafi to help the struggling blacks of this country.

It seems very strange that Muammar Qaddafi has sponsored terrorism and has been implicated in so many bombings, yet the United States has done nothing to kill him or replace him. Qaddafi has been in power for thirty-six years, yet the United States could not remove him—or is it because the CIA put him in power to carry out terrorism to give Islam a bad name and create enemies for Muslims? No leader in the world can hang on to power for thirty-six years without the blessing of the CIA.

UAE

United Arab Emirates formed a federation in 1971 after it gained independence from Britain. It's a federation of seven states: Abu Dhabi, Dubai Sharpiea, Ajmar Fayairah, Ras al'-Khaimah, and Umm-al-Qaiwain. Sheikh Zayed lein Sultan Al Nahyan was the ruler of the UAE since 1971 until his death in 2004. He was succeeded by his son. UAE has a population of about 4 million. More than half are foreign nationals. UAE signed a military defense agreement with the United States in 1994. It relies heavily on the United States for its security. More than 50 percent of the population is South Asian, especially Hindus from India. Hindi is a major language, and in Dubai they built the biggest Hindu temple next to the biggest mosque in Dubai. UAE is an oil-rich country and the third-largest producer of oil in the Gulf region. It has a GDP of $25,200 per capita. The large influx of Hindus from India is consistent with the US policy. The CIA wants the presence of Hindus in every Muslim country to destabilize the society. They get the best jobs and usually run all the technical work.

YEMEN

Yemen has a long history of upheaval and violence. Its per-capita GDP is little over $500. South Yemen was ruled as British India until 1937. With a population of nearly 20 million, North Yemen and South Yemen finally unified in 1990 as Yemen Arab Republic. Since 1962, there has been violence in Yemen. Egypt sent troops to fight the forces loyal to Ahmed's son Badr. Saudi Arabia and Jordan sent troops to fight for Badr. The Saudi forces were backed by the British. In 1967, there were massive riots that killed thousands of people, which continued for a long time despite British intervention. The British finally left, and Yemen got closer to the Soviet Union. Soviet Union Naval Forces had access to the port of Yemen. In 1994, civil war broke out, and southern leaders declared secession, which was eventually repressed as it failed to gain acceptance from the international community. Although Yemen is relatively a poor country, there are a large number of Indian Hindus present. Yemen's history since 1918 has been of violence and upheavals. In October of 2000, the USS *Cole* was attacked by terrorists, killing seventeen US sailors. (It was later attributed to Osama Bin Laden's Al-Qaeda.) This is consistent with the US policy of keeping a region in turmoil and blaming and creating enemies for the Muslim world.

LEBANON

Lebanon became independent in 1943. About 70 percent of Lebanon's population is Muslim. In the beginning, Lebanon was peaceful, and Beirut was the center for finance and trade. All of that changed when the Syrian regime wanted more concessionary deals from Tapline. In 1948, it became a major problem for Aramco. The CIA arranged a coup in Syria in which Colonel Hussne Zaim assured power and trade. All of that changed after the 1948 Arab-Israeli War. More than 110,000 Palestinian refugees moved into Lebanon. After the 1967 Arab-Israeli War, more Palestinians arrived in Lebanon. Palestinians were also ousted from Jordan. They moved to Lebanon, including Yasser Arafat and the PLO.

By 1975 there were over three hundred thousand Palestinians in Lebanon. This caused tensions between Christian and Muslim communities. The Muslims were supportive of the Palestinians, and the Maronite Christians were opposed to the Palestinians. Eventually Egyptian President Gamel Abdal Nasser negotiated a settlement in 1969. However, in 1975 civil war broke out, and the Maronite Christians asked for Syrian intervention. In the meantime, the PLO-Israeli exchanges continued, which caused Israeli support for the Christian militia and Soad Haddad' South Lebanon Army. In 1982, Israel invaded Lebanon and reached Beirut. The PLO and Yasser Arafat negotiated to withdraw from Lebanon. However, this led to a PLO evacuation, but Palestinian refugees remained. On September 1, Israeli troops and Maronite Christian Phalange forces entered the refugee camps of Asabra and Shatilla and massacred more than eight hundred Palestinian refugees who were unarmed civilians and had no connection with the PLO.

There was fighting between Shi'a Muslim militia who wanted the Palestinians out of Lebanon. The Palestinians, leftists, and Druze fighters allied against the Shiite Muslims' Amal Militia, and this led to further Syrian intervention. In 1988, violent clashes erupted between the Amal and Hezbollah. In 1991 a car bomb exploded in a Muslim neighborhood, killing thirty and injuring many others.

Syria's troop deployment in Lebanon was legitimized by the Taif Agreement. The Lebanese Civil War has ended, and Lebanon is beginning to reconstruct itself.

IRAN

I ran is the sixth-largest Muslim country in the world, with a population of about 70 million and per-capita income of $7,000.

Iran's modern history began with the constitutional revolution against the shah in 1905 and the discovery of oil in 1908. In 1921, Reza Khan, an army officer, staged a coup and established a military dictatorship. In 1925, he installed himself as the monarch ruler of Iran and began the Pahlavi dynasty. He was mainly aided by the British. During his sixteen-year rule, he began to modernize Iran. In September of 1941, he handed over power to his son, Mohammed Reza Shah Pahlavi, who ruled Iran until 1979. During World War II, the US and Allied forces used Iran to supply the Soviets.

In 1951 Mohammed Mosaddegh was elected prime minister. He was a nationalist. He immediately nationalized the British-owned oil industry. The British resented this and put an economic blockade on Iran, causing Iran's economy to virtually collapse. Mosaddegh was thrown out of power in 1952 but quickly returned to power in an election, winning with an overwhelming majority. Mosaddegh wanted Iran to profit from its vast oil resources.

The CIA undermined Mosaddegh's government by bribing influential officials, printing false reports in newspapers, and provoking street violence and demonstrations. The shah went into exile. In 1953 the CIA engineered a coup, ousting Mosaddegh, and put the shah back in power. In return the shah allowed the international consortium of British (40 percent) American (40 percent),

French (6 percent), and Dutch (14 percent) representatives to run the Iranian oil companies for the next twenty-five years. The profits were to be shared equally. Therefore Iran had no control over its own resources.

Iran began to establish closer relations with the West, especially the United States. The CIA trained the SAVAK, the shah's secret police. The SAVAK is known to have killed more than thirteen thousand and tortured more than one hundred thousand during the shah's rule. In 1962–63, the shah initiated what is known as the White Revolution, which consisted of land reform, women's rights, and workers' rights. These reforms were criticized by Ayatollah Khomeini, who was arrested and later exiled.

During and after the Arab-Israeli War, Iran did not use oil as a weapon and did not join the Arab oil embargo against the United States, Europe, Japan, and Israel. The shah took advantage of the increased oil revenue due to an increase in oil prices. He was rapidly modernizing Iran. There was growing discontent among the religious leaders over rapid westernization of Iran. The SAVAK repressed any resentment with torture and brutality of the opponents. The shah became unpopular very quickly, and martial law was declared in September of 1978. The shah realized the end of his dynasty had come and fled Iran in January 1970. At the same time the shah of Iran was deposed in Iran, the CIA put Saddam Hussein in power in Iraq.

On November 4, 1970, militant Iranian students seized the US Embassy in Tehran, taking fifty-two American hostages. The Carter administration broke off all diplomatic relations and began an economic boycott. In April of 1980, an American rescue mission was aborted after all the American helicopters had mechanical problems and a mid-air collision killed eight Americans. The hostage crisis was resolved after Reagan accepted all of Iran's demands.

However, in the meantime, the CIA gave the green light to

Saddam Hussein of Iraq to invade Iran. In September 1980, the United States and its allies supplied Iraq with weapons and technology. At the same time, Reagan's administration sold weapons and spare parts to Iran covertly. This is known as the Iran-Contra affair. This is consistent with US policy to keep two Muslim countries fighting each other and drain their resources. The bloody war ended in 1988 with UN Resolution 598.

In 1989 Ayatollah Khomeini died, and Ayatollah Ali Khomeini was his successor. He was soon succeeded by Ali Aubar Rafsanjani, who sought better relations with the West. In 1993 Rafsanjani was reelected. In 1995, the United States suspended all trade with Iran, accusing it of supporting terrorists and attempting to develop nuclear weapons. In 1997 Mohammed Khatami was elected as president. He is a liberal Muslim. The United States is trying to find excuses to isolate Iran. Iran has every right to develop nuclear weapons to defend itself. It has the right to prepare its defenses so it does not become another Iraq or Afghanistan.

TURKEY

Turkey became an independent republic in 1923 with Mustafa Kemal Ataturk as its founding president. He was reelected for several terms beginning in 1927, 1931, and 1935. Although Turkey is 99 percent Muslim, Kemal followed a policy of secular westernization. Kemal ruled Turkey as a virtual dictator, and his Republican People's Party was the only legal party. During his rule, Turkey went through transformation that changed the religious life, social life, and cultural fares. In 1925, the government embarked on an anti-religious policy that prohibited polygamy and wearing of the traditional fez, and in 1926, Swiss, German, and Italian codes of law were imposed. Islam was no longer the state religion.

By the time of Kemal's death in 1938, Turkey had become a state of the Western model. Kemal wanted to make Turkey self-sufficient, without any foreign aid. From the very inception of Turkey, it maintained close relations with the West, especially with Britain and the United States. Turkey became a full member of the North Atlantic Treaty Organization (NATO) in 1952, and immediately US air and missile bases were established in Izonier and Adana.

Turkey shares its borders with Syria, Iraq, and Iran. The close relations between Turkey and the United States are based on an agreement signed in 1947. The United States has given Turkey more than $12.5 billion in economic aid and more than $14 billion in military aid. There is a close relationship, especially between the US and

Turkish militaries. Following Turkish inclusion in the NATO in 1954, Mederas's government returned to power. The government failed to invoke sound economic policies, which led to economic crisis. There was growing opposition and discontent over restrictive laws, which eventually led to unrest and student demonstrations, which eventually led to a coup by General Cemal Gursel in 1962. Medaras and several hundred other Democratic Party leaders were arrested and executed.

General Gursel was following policies dictated by the United States. In 1962, during the Cuban Missile Crisis, the Soviet Union wanted US bases in Turkey to close in return for Soviet bases in Cuba, but Turkey was firmly opposed, and thus the US-Turkey friendship was reaffirmed. General Gursel died in 1966, and Cendet Sunay became the new president. In 1969 the United States and Turkey signed a military agreement that provided for a number of US troops and weapons that the United States would deploy in Turkey. Turkey maintained its good relationship with the United States but at the same time pursued establishing good relations with the Soviet Union. Between 1975 and 1980 Demiral and Ecenit took turns as heads of the government. During their terms, political, special, and economic conditions worsened. In 1980, Gen. Kenan Evren took control of the government and restored order by using force. Under his leadership, a new constitution was approved establishing a unicameral legislature and a provision for General Evren to remain president. The constitution gave the military significant influence over civilian matters and autonomy in deciding military affairs.

In 1983, the conservative Motherland Party won the election, and Turgut Ozal became prime minister. In 1987 martial law was lifted. In 1989 Ozal succeeded General Evren as president. During the Persian Gulf War of 1991, Turkey granted permission to the US forces to launch air strikes against Iraq from Turkish soil. President Ozal died in 1993. Demirel became president, and Tansu Ciller became prime minister (the first woman to hold the post). The Turkish economy was faced with very high inflation of 80 to 90 percent.

In December 1995, the Welfare Party had owned the largest single share in the election (Islamist Party). It formed a coalition government known as the Welfare-True Path Coalition. The leader of the Welfare Party, Necmettin Erbakan, became prime minister, thus ending seventy-five years of secular rule. Erbakan wanted to establish good relations with Libya and Iran and embarked on a path of Muslim education and culture. This caused an alarm for the secular military. The military forced him to resign in 1997. In 1998 the Welfare Party was banned, and its leader, Erbakan, was banned from politics for five years. It is apparent that the politics and government of Turkey have been dominated by Turkish military from the very inception of Turkey. Turkey has been constantly faced with high inflation of 80 to 90 percent that continued into the late 1990s. Although 99 percent of the population of 69 million is Muslims, Islam has no role in Turkey's politics or cultural life.

The Virtue Party was banned by the Turkish high court in 2001 because it is pro-Islamic and anti-secular. In the 2002 election, the Justice and Development Party won a landslide victory, and in 2003 Recep Tayyip Erdogan became the prime minister of Turkey. Turkey is seeking membership in the European Union. In March of 2003, the parliament in Turkey refused to grant permission to US troops to invade Iraq from Turkish soil because the Turkish people did not favor invasion of Iraq. US-Turkish relations were strained.

The US policy of suppressing Muslims and weakening Muslim countries and to deprive them of progress and technology continues. Although Turkey is seeking to become a member of the European Union, it is still considered a developing country. Its technology and industrialization is far behind any European country; it is behind even most Asian countries. Turkey has always been run according to the will and policies of the United States. Only now the United States is contemplating using Turkey as its base to hit targets in Iran and Syria. Recently in 2005 the heads of the FBI and CIA visited Turkey with this proposal. They discussed sharing intelligence and the impact of military action against Iran. Their visit was followed by Israeli Army Chief General Dan Habutz. They also discussed Syria, Iraq, and Iran. Turkey, in spite of being a Muslim country, has always maintained good relations with Israel. The US policy of destroying Muslims continues, and it is apparent they intend to use Israel as their ally to attack Iran and Syria. The visit of the head of the FBI and CIA followed by the Israeli general was disclosed by the German press.

The US decision to hit targets in Iran is based on the fact that Iran supports Al-Qaeda and is trying to develop nuclear weapons. The CIA and its international network plans the Al-Qaeda terrorist network and every terrorist attack. The CIA creates them to get American public support destroying Muslim countries. If the United States has the right to have nuclear weapons (this is the only country that has used nuclear weapons against humanity), then every country has the right to develop nuclear weapons to defend itself, specifically the Muslim countries. Iran has every right to develop nuclear weapons. Otherwise, it will have to be a puppet of the United States, just like every Muslim country at the present time.

SUDAN

S udan is a country with a population of a little over 40 million, and about 65 percent of the population is Muslim. Sudan gained its independence in January of 1956. The northern part of Sudan is predominantly Muslim, while most of the others, including Christians, live in the south. Since the very beginning of Sudan, the south was not granted much autonomy, which sparked a civil war that lasted for seventeen years, from 1955 to 1972.

Sudan faced economic problems, and the government administration was ineffective. In 1958 General Ibrahim Abboud took over power in a bloodless coup. In 1962 the civil war was severe in the southern, mainly Christian parts of Sudan. General Abboud failed on his promise to return Sudan to civilian rule. There was political unrest, massive demonstrations, and riots that eventually forced the military to give up power. After General Abboud, there were several civilian governments that were unable to cope with the economic problems and factionalism and could not agree on a constitution. The governments were dominated by Arab Muslims.

There was growing dissatisfaction among the people, which resulted in a second military coup that put Colonel Gaafar Nimeiry in power. He immediately abolished the parliament and banned all political parties. In 1972 a peace agreement was signed in Addis Ababa that granted southern Sudan self-governance. In 1978 vast quantities of oil were found in southern Sudan, which escalated the strife between north and south. In 1983, Nimeiry introduced Sharia law for Sudan, which met resistance, especially in the south. This caused civil war to break out in the south.

The southern forces of the Sudan People's Liberation Movement were led by John Garang. In 1985, Gaafar Nimeiry was removed from power by General Dhahab. General Dhahab allowed a civilian government to form. However, the civilian government did not function well. In 1989 Gen. Al Bashir took power in a military coup. The civil war in the south continued. In 1995, the Sudanese government was accused of attempting to kill President Mubarak of Egypt, and the UN imposed sanctions on Sudan.

In 1998, the United States launched a missile attack on targets in Sudan, especially in Khartown, which was assumed to have been producing chemical weapons in cooperation with the Al-Qaeda terrorist network. Many civilians were killed, and Sudan denied all accusations. This shows more utmost disregard on the part of the United States, which carries on such missions simply to create chaos and instability in Muslim countries. During the same year, Sudan got a new constitution. In 1999, Sudan began to export its oil. In 2001, hunger and famine in Sudan affected 3 million people. Meanwhile, the civil war in the south continues, and there were systematic killings in Darfur in southern Sudan.

From the time of independence, the Sudanese army was trained and equipped by the British. After the 1967 Arab-Israeli War, relations with the West were cut off. After that it was the Soviet Union and Eastern Bloc countries that sold arms to Sudan. China was also a major supplier.

Sudan's political condition is consistent with what the United States desires in a Muslim majority country. The country has been ruled mostly by military dictators, and the economy remains stagnant, with no progress at all. On the other hand, the United States has threatened to take action against Sudan if the Darfur problem is not resolved. I have reason to believe the CIA created the Darfur problem to find an excuse to further isolate Sudan.

ALGERIA

J ust like any other Muslim country, Algeria had its share of instability and violence and a government usually dominated by the military—the CIA's usual connection. Algeria has a population almost 33 million, and 99 percent are Muslim. It became an independent from France on July 5, 1962. Ahmed Ben Bella was formally elected president in 1963. However, he could not remain long in office. Ben Bella was removed from office in a bloodless coup by Colonel Havari Boumedienne in 1965. Boumedienne was determined to end corruption and is credited for building modern Algeria.

Boumedienne introduced a new constitution in 1976, affirmed his pledge for Socialism, and declared the National Liberation Front (FLN) as the only political party. Boumedienne favored a policy of rapid industrialization. In 1978 Boumedienne died and was replaced by Colonel Chadli Benjedid. Colonel Chadli was reelected in 1984 and 1988. A new constitution was introduced in 1989 and allowed the formation of political parties besides the FLN. Prior to that, in 1986, rapid inflation and unemployment led to strikes and violent demonstrations. This serious civil war continued.

As the ban on political parties was lifted, the Islamic Salvation Front (FIS) was founded and in 1990 won majority in local elections. Afraid that the Islamic Salvation Front (FIS) might win the majority in a parliamentary election, the election was postponed until 1991, and changes were made to the electoral system. This met with resistance from the Islamic Salvation Front, and Algeria found itself caught in a cycle of violence that led to murders, demonstrations, and assassinations, and a civil war broke out. This eventually led to the arrest of FIS leaders Abassi Madani and Ali Belhadj. In December 1991, the Islamic Salvation Front owned 188 seats in parliamentary elections and had an absolute majority. However, the military took over the government and did not allow the Islamic Salvation Front to come to power. Muhammed Boudiaf took over as president. Street gatherings were banned. Violent clashes began beginning another civil war. In 1992 President Boudiaf was assassinated, allegedly by one of his body guards with a link to the Islamists.

In 1994, Colonel Zeroual was appointed president and in 1995 won the election for a five-year term. During the civil war that started in the eighties and lasted well into the nineties, more than one hundred thousand Algerians lost their lives. In 1999 the military supported Abdelaziz Bouteflika, and he won the presidential election when all other candidates pulled out, accused of electoral frauds. In the same year, a referendum approved Bouteflika's law on civil concord, which pardoned all members of the Islamic Salvation Army (AIS), an armed wing of the Islamic Salvation front (FIS).

However, violence did not disappear. Attacks on civilians and security forces continued, and in 2001 violence erupted when a clash between security forces and demonstrators killed hundreds of demonstrators. In 2002, Prime Minister Ali Banfli's National Liberation Front won the election. In 2004, President Bouteflika was reelected as president for a second term. Algeria, ever since its independence, had been plagued by constant violence, civil war, and turmoil. Security forces were responsible for the disappearance of more than six thousand Algerian citizens. The country's president has been dominated by the military, which is CIA's main link in all Muslim countries. Algeria's history of turbulence and violence is consistent with CIA's policy of keeping the Muslim country unstable and depriving them of progress.

In July 2001, President Bouteflika visited the White House, and relations between Algeria and the United States are good. Secretary of State Colin Powell visited Algeria in December 2003. In 2004 direct US investment in Algeria amounted to over $4.1 billion, mostly in the petroleum sector and some in finance and banking. The United States has established an International Military Education Program to train Algerian military personnel. There is staff exchange between the two sides, and Algeria hosted senior US military officials.

AFGHANISTAN

fghanistan became independent in August of 1919. Currently it has a population of about 29 million; 99 percent are Muslims. Habibullah was the first head of state, but he was assassinated during the same year and was succeeded by his son, Amanullah. The British had too much presence and influence, and in 1921 the third Anglo-Afghan War took place. The British were defeated, and Afghanistan got full control of its foreign affairs. In 1929, Amanullah was overthrown, and Nadic Khan became the king. Nadir Khan put down all pro-Amanullah uprisings ruthlessly and abandoned Amanullah's policy of modernizing Afghanistan.

Nadir Khan was assassinated in 1933, and his son Zahir Khan inherited the throne. His prime minister, Daoud, seized power in a military coup in 1973, with the help of the Soviets. Daoud Khan abolished the monarchy and declared himself the president. However, in 1978 Daoud Khan was killed in a bloody coup, and Nar Mohammed Taraki became the new president. Taraki removed all his opponents by mass arrests, torture, and executions. Taraki signed a treaty of friendship with the Soviet Union, thereby allowing Soviet advisors to enter Afghanistan and make policy decisions. There was growing opposition to Soviet and Communist influence in Afghanistan. The CIA got involved. According to a 1998 interview with Zbigniew Brzezinski, the national security advisor of the Carter administration, the CIA established links with Osama bin Laden, a Saudi national. Osama bin Laden became the CIA's link to oppose and to provide resistance to the pro-Soviet government with the intention that this would lead to a Soviet invasion of Afghanistan and its destruction as a nation.

It was the intention of the CIA and the United States for the Soviets to invade Afghanistan. By this time, Hafizullah Amin had seized power and refused to take Soviet advice, thereby leading to the Soviet invasion of December 1979. Hafizullah Amin was executed, and Babrak Karmal became the new prime minister. The Mayaheedeen (freedom fighters) began their fight with the Soviets. The United States, along with Pakistan, continued to supply arms and training to the Mayaheedeen. In 1986, Karmal was replaced by Mohammed Najibullah—former chief of the Afghan secret police—who was known for his brutal tactics of repression.

However, continued support from the United States, Saudi Arabia, and Pakistan led to heavy casualties. The Soviet Union lost forty thousand to fifty thousand troops, and almost one million Afghans lost their lives. The irony of the fact is that it was the United States that wanted the Soviets to invade Afghanistan, and it was the United States that provided support to the Afghan freedom fighters. The United States wanted the fighting to go on so Afghanistan would be destroyed as a nation. Finally the Geneva Accord provided for the return of the Afghan refugees and full Soviet withdrawal from Afghanistan by February 15, 1989. However, the Mayaheedeen continued their fight against the government of Najibullah. The civil war continued even after the Soviet withdrawal. In 1992 the Mayaheedeen took control of Kabul and removed Najibullah from power. Professor Burhanuddin Rabbani was elected president. The US and CIA's involvement continued.

The United States through Pakistan created another group of rebels who were educated mostly in Madrashas in Pakistan, the group called the Taliban. The Taliban came to power with US and Pakistani help and removed President Rabbani in 1996. The Taliban immediately began to repress especially to the women. They began a rule of terror, massive arrests, and mass murders; women were asked to wear the veil and could not go out without a male companion. Males were required to grow beards. In 1998, the Taliban massacred thousands of civilians. The Taliban provided shelter to Osama bin Laden, a Saudi national who was a CIA agent and fought with the Mayaheedeen against the Soviets.

There have been many connections between the Bush Republicans and Osama bin Laden for twenty years. The history of BCCI bank was closely tied to US and Pakistani intelligence. Osama bin Laden's father named Houston investment broker James R. Bath as the business representative of Osama bin Laden in Texas immediately after Bush became the CIA director in 1976. There is a connection here between the CIA, the Taliban, and India. The Bush administration was eager to help India meet its needs for power. President Bush influenced Enron to build a power plant in Dabhal, near Bombay in India, for $3 billion in 2001. Enron was to supply the plant with cheap gas from Qatar and Turkmenistan. They were to build a pipeline from Turkmenistan through Afghanistan, Pakistan, and into India at a cost of $2 billion. It was to serve this purpose that the United States put the Taliban in power.

By this time it is accused that Osama bin Laden, a former CIA agent, had turned into a terrorist and gone against the United States. This is what the CIA wants the American public to believe, whereas in reality the CIA has asked Osama bin Laden to become a terrorist so the United States and the world can accuse Muslims of being terrorists. Osama bin Laden has been a CIA asset since 1976, when Bush became the director of the CIA. Following the September attack on the World Trade Center in 2001, in October 2001 the United States invaded Afghanistan to look for Osama bin Laden.

It is amazing that it took the United States, with all its intelligence, so long to find Osama bin Laden. You would have to be a fool to believe that. After the US invasion, Hamid Karzai became president of Afghanistan. Hamid Kazai, the American choice, was later elected as president in 2004. It was the United States that put the Taliban in power in 1996, and it was the United States that put the Taliban out of power in 2001. What the United States wants is an unstable Muslim country that will destroy itself and progress and development. The Americans have no business in Afghanistan, yet US occupation of Afghanistan continues with the excuse that they are looking for Al-Qaeda members and Osama bin Laden.

MALAYSIA

Malaysia is a country with a population of 25 million, of which about 60 percent are Muslims, 19 percent are Buddhists, 9 percent are Christians, and 6 are percent Hindus. It got its independence on August 31, 1957. About 25 percent of the population is Chinese. Tunku Abdul Rahman became the first prime minister of Malaysia. At the time, 75 percent of the Muslims were below poverty line in Malaysia. The economy and businesses were controlled by the Chinese and Indians. The education act of 1961 required that Malay and English would be only medium of instruction and the university entry examination would be in Malay only. This was an attempt to give the Malay an opportunity to catch up with the Chinese and Indians, who had an advantage in education.

The United Malay National Organization (UMNO) government had an agenda to shift economic power from the Chinese to the Malay. In 1970, 75 percent of the Malaysians who lived below poverty line were Muslim Malays. The policies of the government caused the Chinese to go for education in Singapore, Australia, Britain, and the United States. The Chinese were disproportionately powerful in Malaysia's economy. However, by 2000, that gradually shifted, and Malays were also getting into owning and managing businesses.

After Tunku Abdul Rahman resigned in September 1970, Tim Abdul Razak became the prime minister. He initiated the new economic policy, which was to eliminate poverty and eliminate economic functions with the race. In January of 1976, Tun Hussein leim Dato became the third prime minister of Malaysia. The fourth prime minister of Malaysia was Dr. Mahather Bin Mohammad, and he had the longest tenure. He became prime minister 1981 and ruled until 2003. Dr. Mahathir followed a policy to bridge the gap between ethnic divisions. He created many opportunities for women. He maintained good relations with the United States and India.

India and Malaysia have signed several agreements, including the cultural agreement of 1978, Cooperation in Science and Technology in 1998, a trade agreement in 2000, and the exemption of the visa requirement for holders of diplomatic and official passports in 2001. They have also signed many memoranda of understanding. Dr. Mahalhir Mohammed made six visits to India during his twenty-two years as prime minister. In 2004 Prime Minister Abdullah Ahmad Badawi also visited India. There has been a great deal of cooperation in trade and commerce between Malaysia and India. There are fifty-seven Indian joint ventures in Malaysia, ranging from palm oil refining, power, railways, civil construction, training, and information technology. Malaysians of Indian origin prefer to study professional courses in India. Hindus are only 6 percent of the population, but about 34 percent of all doctors and lawyers are Indians. There are almost 2 million Indians in Malaysia. Just like most of the Muslim countries, Indians have penetrated Malaysia for a long time.

This has been the history of every Muslim country. The CIA has been involved in creating turmoil in every Muslim country, and the CIA has succeeded in allowing Hindus to penetrate in all Muslim countries.

CIA AND THE DRUG CONNECTION

During the forty years of the Cold War, the CIA joined hands with gangsters and warlords who were drug dealers to fight communism and to launch covert operations. From Turkey to Thailand, in Burma during the 1950s, in Laos during the 1970s, and in Afghanistan during the 1980s, the CIA allied with major drug dealers to attain their objective of mobilizing armies against the Soviet Union and China.

In order to gain their support, the CIA allowed the warlords to cultivate opium, process it, and ship it to the United States. The CIA battled communists in Laos by allowing the Honong officers to load opium on the CIA's carrier Air America. There were twenty-one opium refineries in the golden triangle of Burma, Thailand, and Laos, and the CIA had full knowledge of their operations. These areas were under the control of CIA allies Nam Kung and Ban Houei Sai. By 1971, 34 percent of all soldiers in South Vietnam were heroin addicts and were supplied by dealers who were CIA allies. When there was revolt against the leftist Sandanista government in Nicaragua, the CIA hired Colonel Enrique Bermudez to organize the Contra guerilla army. Bermudez accepted funds from two Nicaraguan exiles who were cocaine dealers.

When the United States moved into Afghanistan to support the Mayaheedeen, the CIA supported the opium growers in Afghanistan.

OIL DIPLOMACY

There is a direct link between terrorism and oil. In 1953 British interests were hampered when elected the prime minister of Iran, Mossadegh, demanded a bigger share for his countrymen of the exploited oil. The British, along with Kermit Roosevelt of the CIA, overthrew Mossaddegh's government and installed the shah of Iran.

The British concentrated the Jews in Palestine to form the state of Israel to keep the Arabs, who were soaked with oil, off balance. This is the British policy of divide and rule.

There is conclusive evidence that Osama bin Laden and other Islamic militant networks were harbored by the CIA as part of Washington's foreign policy. The CIA admits that Osama bin Laden, a Saudi, was one of the CIA's intelligence assets but has now gone against the CIA. This is hard to believe. The CIA wants Osama bin Laden to carry out terrorist acts so the Muslims can be blamed for terrorism.

WHY MUSLIMS HATE AMERICA

1947–48	Palestine was partitioned, and the state of Israel was created. Palestinians were expelled from their own homeland.
1947	The CIA organized a military coup in Syria, deposing an elected government.
1953	The CIA overthrew the elected government of Iran and put the shah of Iran in power, which led to a quarter century of regressive and dictatorial rule.
1956	The United States refused to go on with the promised funding of the Aswan Dam in Egypt because Egypt got arms from the Eastern Bloc.
1956	Israel, Britain, and France invaded Egypt.
1957	US troops landed in Lebanon.
1960	The CIA made an unsuccessful attempt to assassinate Iraqi leader Abdul Karim Qassim.
1963	The CIA staged a coup, bringing the Bath party, soon to be headed by Sadaam Hussein, into power in Iraq and asked them to kill so-called communists.
1967	The United States vetoed Security Council Resolution 242, which called for Israel to withdraw from territories captured in 1967 war.
1970	Civil war between Jordan and PLO broke out. The United States and Israel took the side of Jordan, and Syria backed the PLO.
1973	The United States took the side of Israel in the war against the Arabs.
1975	The United States vetoed a UN Security Council resolution condemning Israel for the massacres in Palestinian refugee camps in Lebanon.

1978–79	The United States tried to save the shah in Iran but failed.
1979–88	The United States began covert aid to the Mayaheedeen six months before the Soviet invasion. This provoked the Soviets to invade Afghanistan.
1980–88	The United States provoked Saddam Hussein to invade Iran. The United States opposed the UN Security Council's action to condemn the invasion. US arms were allowed to be transferred to Iraq. At the same time, the United States supplied arms to Iran through Israel, thereby arming both sides to continue the war.
1983	There were terrorist bombings of US Marine barracks in Lebanon in which hundreds of US citizens died. Explosives were used, which were exclusively used by the CIA.
1982	The United States gave the green light to Israel to invade Lebanon, which killed seventeen thousand civilians. The United States vetoed several UN Security Council resolutions condemning the invasion.
1987–92	Israel used US arms to repress Palestinians. The United States vetoed five UN Security Council resolutions condemning Israel.
1987	The United States vetoed UN Security Council resolutions condemning Israeli repression in Lebanon.
1990–91	The United States gave Saddam Hussein green light to invade Kuwait.

MUSLIMS AND TERRORISM

The Bush administration claimed that behind the tragic events of September 11, 2001, were caused by Saudi terrorist Osama bin Laden. Therefore, President Bush launched a major war supposedly against international terrorism. There is ample evidence that confirms agencies of US government, including the CIA, harbored Islamic militant networks as part of Washington's foreign policy agenda. In Afghanistan, they are targeting training camps, which were established by the CIA in the 1980s. [16],[17]

Because of evidence, the CIA no longer can deny that Osama bin Laden is a CIA agent who has now gone against the CIA. This is difficult to believe, because if the CIA wants to find Osama bin Laden, they should have no problem. This is simply a fabrication. The evidence is overwhelming that the CIA never severed its ties to the "Islamic militant network." The CIA does not only maintain links, but the operation has also become more sophisticated. Pakistan's military and intelligence operations are controlled by the CIA and were used during the Afghan War. Throughout the 1990s, the Pakistan Inter-Services Intelligence (ISI) was used by the CIA

---

16 Michel Chossudovsky, "Clinton Administration Supported the 'Militant Islamic Base,'" http://www.nadir.org/nadir/initiativ/agp/free/chossudovsky/islamicbase.htm

17 Michel Chossudovsky, "Cover-up or Complicity of the Bush Administration? The Role of Pakistan's Military Intelligence (ISI) in the September 11 Attacks," http://www.ratical.org/ratville/CAH/CHO111A.html

to supply weapons in the civil war in Yugoslavia according to report
of the London-based International Media Corporation.

> Reliable sources report that the United States is
> now [1994] actively participating in the arming and
> training of the Muslim forces of Bosnia-Herzegovina
> in direct contravention of the United Nations accords.
> US agencies have been providing weapons made in
> China (PRC), North Korea (DPRK) and Iran with
> the knowledge and agreement of the US Government,
> supplied the Bosnian forces with a large number
> of multiple rocket launchers and a large quantity of
> ammunition. These included 107mm and 122mm
> rockets from the PRC and VBR-23- multiple rocket
> launchers ... made in Iran ... It was (also) reported
> that 400 members of the Iranian Revolutionary
> Guard (Pasdaran) arrived in Bosnia with a large
> supply of arms and ammunition. It was alleged that
> the US Central Intelligence Agency (CIA) had full
> knowledge of the operation that the CIA believed
> that some of the 400 had been detached for future
> terrorist operations in Western Europe ... The US
> administration has not restricted its involvement to the
> clandestine contravention of the UN arms embargo on
> the region ... It [also] committed three high ranking
> delegations over the past two years [Prior to 1994] in
> failed attempts to bring the Yugoslav Government into
> the line with US policy.18

---

18 International Media Corporation Defense and Strategy Policy, "US Commits Forces,
Weapons to Bosnia," London, 31 October 1994.

The US congressional report of 1997 fully agrees with the above quote. The Republican Party Committee (RPC) report accused the Clinton administration of having "helped turn Bosnia into a militant Islamic base." The CIA recruited terrorists from the Muslim world.

> The Republican Party Committee report confirming that the Clinton administration had links to Militant Islamic fundamentalist organizations including Osama bin Laden. While the congressional reports confirmed that the US Government and the CIA was working with Osama bin Laden's Al Qaeda, this link continued with both Clinton and Bush administration. Rep. John Kasich of the House Armed Services Committee said, "We connected ourselves [in 1998-99] with the KLA which was the staging point for Bin Laden.

> In the wake of the tragic events of September 11, Republicans and Democrats in unison have given their full support to the President to wage war on Osama. In 1999, Senator Joe Lieberman had stated authoritatively that 'Fighting for the KLA is fighting for human rights and American values.' In the hours following the October 7 missile attacks on Afghanistan, the same Joe Lieberman called for punitive air strikes against Iraq. 'We're in a war against terrorism ... we can't stop with bin Laden and the Taliban.' Yet Senator Joe Lieberman as a member of the Armed Services Committee of the Senate had access to all the congressional documents

pertaining to KLA-Osama links. In making this
statement, he was fully aware that agencies of the
US Government as well as NATO were supporting
international terrorism.[19]

The Bush administration claimed that it had proof Osama bin Laden
was behind the attack on the WTC and the Pentagon. British Prime
Minister Tony Blair also claimed he had seen conclusive evidence
that Osama bin Laden was behind the September 11 attack. What
they failed to mention was that agencies of the US government, including the CIA, continued to help Osama bin Laden and his Al-
Qaeda. These sorts of events give the United States the opportunity
to occupy Muslim countries like Afghanistan and Iraq.

A major war supposedly against international
terrorism has been launched by a government which is
harboring international terrorism as part of its foreign
policy agenda. In other words, the main justification for
waging war has been totally fabricated. The American
people have been deliberately and consciously mislead
by their government into supporting a major military
adventure which affects our collective future ... The
administration confirmed its intention to embark
on a sustained military campaign rather than a single
dramatic action directed against Osama bin Laden.
In addition to Afghanistan, a number of countries in
the Middle East were mentioned as possible targets
including Iraq, Iran, Libya and Sudan.[20]

---

19 CRG, "Osamagate," accessed January 28, 2013, www.globalresearch.ca/articles/
    CHO110A.html.
20 CRG, accessed January 28, 2013, www.globalresearch.ca/articles/ch0110a.html.

WHAT SHOULD THE MUSLIM WORLD DO?

At the present time, none of the Muslim countries have true sovereignty. They have to dance to the American tune. Every Muslim country is controlled by the CIA. Hindus are the greatest threat to Muslims. The CIA has made sure that Hindus penetrate every Muslim country. The CIA will try to push every Muslim country toward India.

None of the Muslim countries have sustained democracy. Most Muslim countries have authoritarian rule. Every Muslim country should try to attain democracy. Pakistan always seems to have a military dictatorship. If the Muslim countries are to be truly sovereign, they first need to be able to defend themselves. It is not necessary that every Muslim country should become a nuclear power. Pakistan is already a nuclear power, and it is imperative that Pakistan remain a strong nuclear power. Second, there has to be a way to assure democracy in Pakistan and keep the military away from politics. Every Muslim country should help Pakistan remain a strong military power. Third, every Muslim country should support Iran in becoming a nuclear power. After that, every Muslim country can have security agreements with Iran and Pakistan, which would guarantee the security of every Muslim country. Muslims need to build up their defenses, not to adventure like America but to defend themselves so we don't have another Iraq or Afghanistan.

Muslims must remember the greatest threat to Islam is America, and the CIA's main allies that are destroying Muslims are India and Israel. Remember, the Hindus of India, especially Hindus of West Bengal, are the CIA's main ally in destroying Muslims. The Hindus have penetrated every Muslim country with the help of the CIA. India's military buildup is directed toward Muslims, especially Pakistan, and Hindus are brutally repressing the Muslims of Kashmir.

Muslims all over the world were shocked when President Khatami of Iran was the chief guest at India's Republic Day celebration in January 2003. How can the leader of a Muslim country be a chief guest to see the display of Indian military might that is directed toward Muslims? If Muslim countries are to remain sovereign, they must build up their nuclear power, and they must have common defenses. To develop the economies of Muslim countries, they must develop a common market. Muslim countries must trade among themselves, and each country should produce what it can produce best. Muslim countries must be prepared so that if they are attacked, like Iraq and Afghanistan, they can give a fitting reply. A true Muslim must not be afraid to fight for the truth. A true Muslim is never an aggressor but must be a mighty defender. The Americans and Indians will try to create divisions among Shiite Muslims and Sunni Muslims. The British have done that historically. The Muslims must be united regardless of whether they are Shiite or Sunni. We are brothers in Islam, and there should be no difference.

MOHAMMED ASHRAFUL HAQUE

I was born on July 9th. 1953 in what was East Pakistan (now Bangladesh). I began my education at Lakeview Preparatory School an English Medium school. My early childhood was spent at Kapasia, Joydevpur, Kaliakor and finally Dhaka. After 2 years at Lakeview preparatory school I transferred to a Bengali Medium school known as New Paltan line high school after that I transferred to West end High school. I finished my sixth grade at west end high school and then I was admitted to Ayub Cadet College in Rajshahi, East Pakistan. This was a boarding school which specifically prepared students to eventually join the defense forces. I have completed 10th grade at Ayub Cadet college and taken the secondary school certificate exam in April of 1970, I was placed in the first division.

After that civil war broke out and there was struggle for the free country of Bangladesh. At the age of 19 I was trained and joined the Liberation Army of Bangladesh. After Bangladesh became independent I transferred to Notre Dame College in Dhaka.

In 1972 I was suddenly put in jail, because I was accused by the Indian Ambassador to Bangladesh to have raped and killed an

Indian Woman. While I was in Jail the case never went to court and I was tried in absentia and ordered to be hanged till death. But the day before I was supposed to be hanged, the Prime Minister of Bangladesh Sheikh Mujibur Rahman ordered to free me because of lack of evidence and because the case never went to court. After my release from Jail I took the Higher Secondary School Certificate Exam and I was placed in the second division. After my H.S.C. exam I was admitted at Dhaka University in the department of Public Administration. At the same time I applied in the Army to join Army commissioned officers. I was selected in the Army. Just before my departure for Army Academy I met a missionary who used to work for Mennonite Central Committee, his name was Ken Koehn. He offered to help me to come to the United States for higher education. I was interested and applied for admission in the United States college. I was accepted at Bethel College in North Newton, Kansas. Mr. Maynard Shelly, who also worked for Mennonite central committee wrote a letter of recommendation to Bethel College about my English Proficiency. So I did no have to take the Toefl or Sat. I arrived at Bethel College on 5th September 1973 at the age of 20. I completed my undergraduate education at Bethel College majoring in Economics and Business Administration in August of 1976. During my school year I worked Part time at a construction firm, Prestressed Concrete and I was also a waiter at a Ramada Inn restaurant. After that I completed My MBA from Ball State University in Muncie, Indiana. After completing My MBA in August of 1978, I taught for four years at Manchester College in North Manchester, Indiana. After that I was admitted at the Doctoral program at Mississippi State University. I received my DBA majoring in Finance and minoring in quantitative analysis and Economics in December of 1985. I was appointed as Assistant professor of Finance at Pittsburg State University in Pittsburg, Kansas from January 1985 till June 1987. After that I looked for employment in Bangladesh and was frequent traveler between Bangladesh and U.S.A till August of 1993. I taught at Illinois College in Jacksonville, Illinois till May of 1998. From June 1998 till May of 2001 I taught at North South University in Dhaka, Bangladesh. I returned to the United States and got employment at Texas A&M University-Texarkana and continue to teach both undergraduate and graduate courses in Finance. Writing this short book about the Muslim World and the CIA is my attempt to bring before the American people, the truth which they should know, and judge for themselves whether it is fair to consider Muslims as terrorists as portrayed by the media and the American Government.

REFERENCES

Gary Allen, *None Dare Call it Conspiracy*. Concord, MA: Concord Press, 1971.

Global Research, "Crimes against Humanity: Routine Torture and Murder in Iraq's Prisons," January 27, 2013, http://www.globalresearch. ca/crimes-against-humanity-routine-torture-and-murder-in-iraqs-prisons/5320703.

www.skolnicksreport.com/boterrorists.html

www.larouchepale.com/other/1995/224/_golden_cresecent.html

www.thirdworldtraveler.com/cia/ciadrug_fallout.html

www.zmag.org/shalomhate.htm

www.stat-usa.gov/miscfiles.nsf/bnotes/
aff430b8f39dc686525703d0066cee

www.stat-usa.gov/miscfiles.nsf/vwcountry/08684FFA507255E5852570
650040A6A

www.stat-usa.gov/miscfiles.nsf/bnotes/4109AFBB4E97326B85257068
003A/883

www.meaindia.nic.in/foreignrelation/malaysia.pdf

http://nerdeka.virtualmalaysia.com/fastfact/Prime_minister.
cfm?sec=1&mnu=3

www.afghan-web.com/history/chron/index3.html

www.com.net.uk/home/nimmann/peace/opium.htm

www.alternet.org/story/12525

www.globalresearch.ca/articles/BRZ110A.html

www.afghan-web.com/history/chron/index4.html

www.ishipress.com/afghans.htm

www.stat-usa.gov/miscfiles.nsf/bnotes/2df12222B9C5A356C85256FE
E0050F0FE

www.geographyiq.com/countries/ag/Algeria_US_relations_Summary.htm

http://news.bbc.co.uk/2/hi/middle_east/country_Profiles/811140.stm

www.stat-usa.gov/miscfiles.nsf/bnotes/204cd66712c5dd4a85256f6900
55FIFA

www.afrol.com/articles/13383

http://crawfurd.dk/africa/sudan_timeline.htm

www.stat-usa.gov/miscfiles.nsf/BNOTES/2AF3BFE372E62F12852570
4C0045BC74

www.uruknet.info/?P=m/18970&1=i+size=1&hd=0

www.turkishweekly.net/news.php?id=24155

www.stat-usa.gov/miscfiles.nsf/BNOTES/421D34AB73CD40A885256
F540053551

www.encyclopedia.com/html/section/turkey_history.asp

www.guardian.co.uk/comment/story/0,3604,1021997,00.html

www.mage.com/tlbody.html

www.stat-usa.gov/miscfiles.nsf/BNOTES/
E3C75D4B9A1B302585256F09004B4B1B

www.encyclopedia.com/html/section/iran_history.asp

www.stat-usa.gov/miscfiles.nsf/
BNOTES522E5496830DC6FD85256F5400534B23?

http://almashriq.hiof.no/lebanon/300/320/327/notes/index.html

www.stat-usa.gov/miscfiles.nsf/BNOTES/5146BE5022A2CF8085256F
16004A3F42

www.infoplease.come/ipa/A0108074.html

www.stat-usa.gov/miscfiles.nsf/BNOTES/2CCB06F2ED4076CA85256
F540053495

http://www.stat-usa.gov/miscfiles.nsf/BNOTES/E-
F46485B59EE62685256F7E00448CF

http://timeline.ws/countries/LIBYA.html

www.Zum.de/whkmla/region/northafrica/Libya.html

www.stat-usa.gov/miscfiles.nsf/BNOTES/616A8B44625C4782285256
F09004B50F5

www.hartford-hwp.com/archives/f1/index-la.html

www.royalty.nu/MiddleEast/Jordan

www.stat-usa.gove/miscfiles.nsf/BNOTES/66ADCD4BED6EOA7F85
25700A004DA

www.hartford-hwp.com/archives/51/218.html

www.stat-usa.gov/misfiles.nsf/BNOTES/
F0FB58B38464065C85256F09004B4CD4

www.mideastweb.org/timeline.htm

www.stat-usa.gov/miscfiles.nsf/BNOTES/
FA70614802865CB185270520057B001

www.zum.de/whkmla/region/norhafrica/tlegyptmod.html

http://www.website1.com/odyssey/week6/FYI.html

www.forham.edu/halsall/mod/balfour.html

www.stat-usa.gov/miscfiles.nsf/BNOTES/3340B14F3D1F0EF385256F
09004B4E17?

www.stat-usa.gov/miscfiles.nsf/BNOTES/17838FF23E7FG92E85256F
FC004011BD?

www.gimonca.com/sejarah/sejarah12.shtml

www.gimonca.com/sejarah/sejarah11.shtml

www.gimonca.com/sejarah/sejarah10.shtml

www.gimonca.com/sejarah/sejarah09.shtml

www.virtualbangladesh.com/history/overview.html

www.saag.org/%5cpapers15%5cpaper.1490.html

www.freerepublic.com/focus/f-news/1439060/posts

www.mtholyoke.edu/acad/intrel/kashun91.htm

www.armyinkashmir.org/v2/his_persp/unresolution_areality.shtml

www.Jammu-Kashmir.com/archives/archives2004/Kashmir20041012b.
html

www.mtholyoke.edu/acad/intrel/Kasun122.htm

http://ess.idrf.org/esms/essayview.php?showessay=show&dipes=129&d
ies=&dips=126&

http://icssa.org/icss%20-%20them_Pakistan_Bangladesh.htm

www.geocities.com/Athens/styx/7297/indexd.htm

www.virtualbangladesh.com/history/Jahanara_iman.html

www.virtualbangladesh.com/history/overview_akram.html

M. Niaz Asadullah "Educational Disparity in Pakistan 1947–71," Univ. of Oxford, April 2004.

Deepa Ollapolly, "US-India Relations: Ties that Bind?" George Washington University.

www.foreignaffairs.org/19790201faessay9906/adam-u/am/U-S-Soviet-relations-umha.

http://opendemocracy.net/forums/thread.jspa?forumID=754&threadID=43498&messageID

www.encylopedia.com/html/section/Arabisra_The1973-74War(Theyomkipperwar).asp

www.encylopedia.com/html/secion/Arabisra_The1967War(TheSix-DayWar).asp

www.jewishvirtuallibrary.org/jsource/US-Israel/Special.html

www.ims.ccsu.edu/media.htm

www.storyofPakistan.com/articletext.asp?article=A069

www.eoijakarta.or.id/Indiandonesia.html

www.indianembassy.org.sa/Pages/IndiaSaudi/FirstPage.htm

Embassy of India, Tripoli, Libya.